New Aesthetic 3

A Collection of Experimental and Independent Type Design

Edited by Leonhard Laupichler & Sophia Brinkgerd

Sorry Press®

EDITORIAL
Design and art are constantly evolving. In both professions, we either risk that our work is transforming into artifacts from a previous period or we can embrace change, encourage experiments and produce more meaningful results. New Aesthetic is looking at experimental and independent type design as an intersection of art and design. Typography has established itself in our graphic work culture as an essential component—whether in print or on screen—serving to strengthen visual messages. The traditional form of type was built around the way we read and write. However, we live in a time of transformation and adaption: Our world is experiencing great changes and our habits shift to accommodate new technologies as they appear. As designers, our creative process mirrors how we use our imagination to shape modern visual communication, it brings in a dash of visual surprise, and breaks the conventions we are used to. What if we saw typography in a more playful context, and not necessarily as a final outcome but rather an experimental process? There is potential in blurring and obfuscating the lines of legibility and practicality, pushing the boundaries of emotional expressiveness and allowing for unusual approaches in modern design. Typographic systems can be read in different ways, and every designer is using different styles and is forming new shapes and meanings for users and readers to interpret. The way typefaces interact with individual words can be considered an art form in itself. New Aesthetic is interested in creating an environment where the expressive side of typography design comes together and strives for original solutions instead of seeking traditional perfection.   The Editors

TYPEFACE
Aerrak

DESIGNER/S
Vince Hegedus

INFORMATION
The idea behind Aerrak was to experiment with combining a sort of renaissance aesthetic and a transitional serif. Most of its letters start out with the characteristics of a transitional serif, while having curved details, for instance in the bowls or crossbars that may remind us of medieval imagery. The main purpose for Aerrak was to break away from the futuristic directions and to create a typeface that could have worked several centuries ago as well as on contemporary platforms. Due to its stylised features it is intended for display use, working best as title text or with shorter sentences.

CLASSIFICATION
Display

STYLES
Regular

RELEASE
2022

CONTACT
@vince_hegedus

THE
BEGINNING OF
A NEW ERA
IN A TIME OF
INEVITABLE
SILENCE

SILENCE
INEVITABLE
IN A TIME OF
A NEW ERA
BEGINNING OF
THE

TYPEFACE
Albator

DESIGNER/S
Stefan Mader, Lynn Cariou

INFORMATION
Munich, 02.02.2022 [21:30:45 – LC] So we've been working on this typeface for quite some time. Did you have any idea what it was going to be called when we started the project? [21:30:53 – SM] Actually, no. [21:31:00 – LC] What are your thoughts about this typeface? What do you feel when you're looking at it? [21:31:08 – SM] It's about mechanics, machines, space ships, engineering, trains, connections, connectivity, masculinity, rhythm, duality, sharpness and geometry. [21:31:29 – LC] That's true. This type is so unique. Somehow it's also about muscles, veins—almost organic in some aspects. But when you reference the space ship, are you referring to the cartoon from my childhood? Albator? Have you heard about him? [21:31:58 – SM] Yes exactly, with a unique scar on his face. The scar almost looks like the ink traps within the typeface.

CLASSIFICATION
Display

STYLES
Regular

RELEASE
2022

CONTACT
stefanmader.com
@stefan.mader
lynncariou.com
@lynn.cariou

CHARACTER OVERVIEW: 186

Ally

Samira Schneuwly

INFORMATION
Ally is an expressive but delicate typeface that pushes the boundaries of legibility. Its unconventional shapes emerged from calligraphic experiments with the attempt to design characters with only one stroke and curves only. To indicate the beginning and end of each line, rather sharp and concise serifs were introduced. Instead of aligning the typeface on a traditional baseline, each individual letter orients itself to its own horizontal centre line. The kerning enables the characters to intertwine and leads to a harmonious and balanced overall appearance. Ally was initially conceived for display situations and short texts but can also evoke interesting textures in smaller sizes and longer texts. It provides a playground for distinctive and vigorous typography.

CLASSIFICATION
Experimental

STYLES
Regular

RELEASE
N/A

CONTACT
samiraschneuwly.ch
@samiraschneuwly

TYPEFACE
Anthony

DESIGNER/S
Sun Young Oh

INFORMATION
Anthony is a display typeface inspired from artworks by British sculptor Anthony Caro. The form of this typeface comes from the visual look and feel of his sculptures. The letters are made solely out of straight lines which are leaning on each other. Anthony developed from an artistic point of view to create letter-like abstract forms, not classical letters. The typeface is packed with stylistic alternates for most letters that are pseudo-randomly picked when you write some text.

CLASSIFICATION
Display

STYLES
Regular

RELEASE
2021

CONTACT
sunyoungoh.com
@sunynoh

UNPERFECT;

Combination
Rhombi

Dimension

Uniform

Symmetry

Ellipsoids
Trapezoids

Arrogant

Carmen Nácher

INFORMATION
Arrogant is my first typeface and it came out of experimenting with different shapes. I first created the letter "a" and then I made the "r" following the same style—and then the name Arrogant came to my mind because both letters where looking very pompous. Next, I decided to create the rest of the word "Arrogant" and post it on Instagram. It was my first type-related post and it got a very good response, after that I left the project a bit aside, and after spending some time focusing my work more and more on type design, I decided to complete the rest of the alphabet, numbers and special characters. Arrogant, just like the rest of my typographic work, is a bold, highly contrasted typeface in which every glyph is following the same style or concept. This is represented visually through repetitive shapes that are on the one hand experimental, but on the other hand respect the traditional weights of each letter so that the typeface can be readable as a whole.

CLASSIFICATION
Display

STYLES
Regular

RELEASE
2022

CONTACT
carmen-nacher.com
@carmen.nacher

Attack Type

Ivan Tsanko

INFORMATION

Attack Type is a first-born character typeface that I've been working on for the last two years. It is inspired by Ukrainian Christian graphic, Heorhiy Narbut, and many other Ukraine historical references. The core character or Attack type is that fonts are like a weapon for peace. I really think that the language we use is our shield. I am from Ukraine. For many years, my language has been destroyed, silenced and hashed up. So for me it is important to rebuild my language and rethink my writing. In 2022, I experience how my letters communicate with people from all around the world and speak up for democracy, peace, and the power of Ukrainian culture.

CLASSIFICATION
Serif

STYLES
Regular
Medium
Bold
Heavy

RELEASE
2022

CONTACT
ivantsanko.com
@ivantsankoo

*translated from ukrainian:
"freedom or death".

Воля або Смерть

Quote by
Nestor Ivanovych Makhno (Father Makhno),
a Ukrainian anarchist revolutionary and
the commander of an independent anarchist
army in Ukraine from 1917 to 1921.

TYPEFACE
Ballo

DESIGNER/S
Anna Khorash

INFORMATION
Ballo is a bold stencil display typeface full of fanciness and jocosity. Apart from the soft design there is a logic of brush pen calligraphy in the base of shapes. A slight reverse contrast emphasises the informal and playful nature of the face. The spacing is balanced to keep the harmony of counter shapes inside and outside the letters. At the same time it lets the eye perceive individual elements of the letter as a whole. The face is equipped with a basic set of light and delicate punctuation that doesn't compete with main characters and adds a vital elegance to the set. The character set includes basic Latin and Cyrillic alphabets. Ballo started from a quick sketch for fun. I had the need to draw something informal, friendly and free from classical text canons and rules. Later it became a kind of mental exercise to complete wobbly forms inside the alphabet. The challenge was to find a logic that functions for all letters of Cyrillic and Latin alphabets while keeping the playful nature.

CLASSIFICATION
Display

STYLES
Stencil Bold

RELEASE
2021

CONTACT
@horashann

Drop of
mercury
Melting point
of zinc 419.5
Congelation
Viscosity
Newtonian
Fluid

Bezier

Chiachi Chao

INFORMATION
Bezier is a friendly display typeface constructed without any straight line. Its letterforms were conceived as the silhouette of three-dimensional sculptural forms inspired by the organic sculptures of Jean Arp, Henry Moore and Isamu Noguchi, which challenges the traditional model of letterform rendered by the trace of nibs. Like the yin-yang symbol, the letterforms of Bezier are defined by the dynamic interplay between the negative and positive space which allows the font setting in tight spacing for the display sizes.

CLASSIFICATION
N/A

STYLES
Regular

RELEASE
2019

CONTACT
chiachichao.com
@chiachi.chao

TYPEFACE
Bijou

DESIGNER/S
Odin Lowsley

INFORMATION
Bijou, "jewel" in French, imitates the sharp cuts of diamonds and other precious gems to produce a display face which—through its contrasting strokes—conveys strength that fortifies fragility. The typeface is constructed from a set of similar shapes and angles, mimicking cut gemstones, as if each glyph has been chiselled by the same tool, creating a sense of visual harmony. Inspired by the aesthetic presentation of the black opal in the Safdie brothers' movie "Uncut Gems" (2019), Bijou is built on a simple grid system and draws a likeness to crude, paper-cut shapes, reflecting the perfection of gems, including their natural imperfections.

CLASSIFICATION
Faceted Display

STYLES
N1

RELEASE
2022

CONTACT
odinlowsley.com
@odin.lowsley

TYPEFACE
Black Mamba

DESIGNER/S
Awista Montagne

INFORMATION
Black Mamba is an experimental display typeface I designed in 2020. It's based on an old calligraphy sketch. It's also a tribute to the basketball player Kobe Bryant aka the Black Mamba. In this experimental typeface, I wanted to merge many properties of the black mamba mentality. This fearless font is unstoppable, it stays focused, is fast, really quick, always dynamic, it is meandering like a snake and moving like a basketball player. Like in most of my works, I wanted to highlight the rhythmic pattern created by the letters instead of being focused on the readability.

CLASSIFICATION
Display

STYLES
Regular

RELEASE
2020

CONTACT
behance.net/awista
@awista_3YK

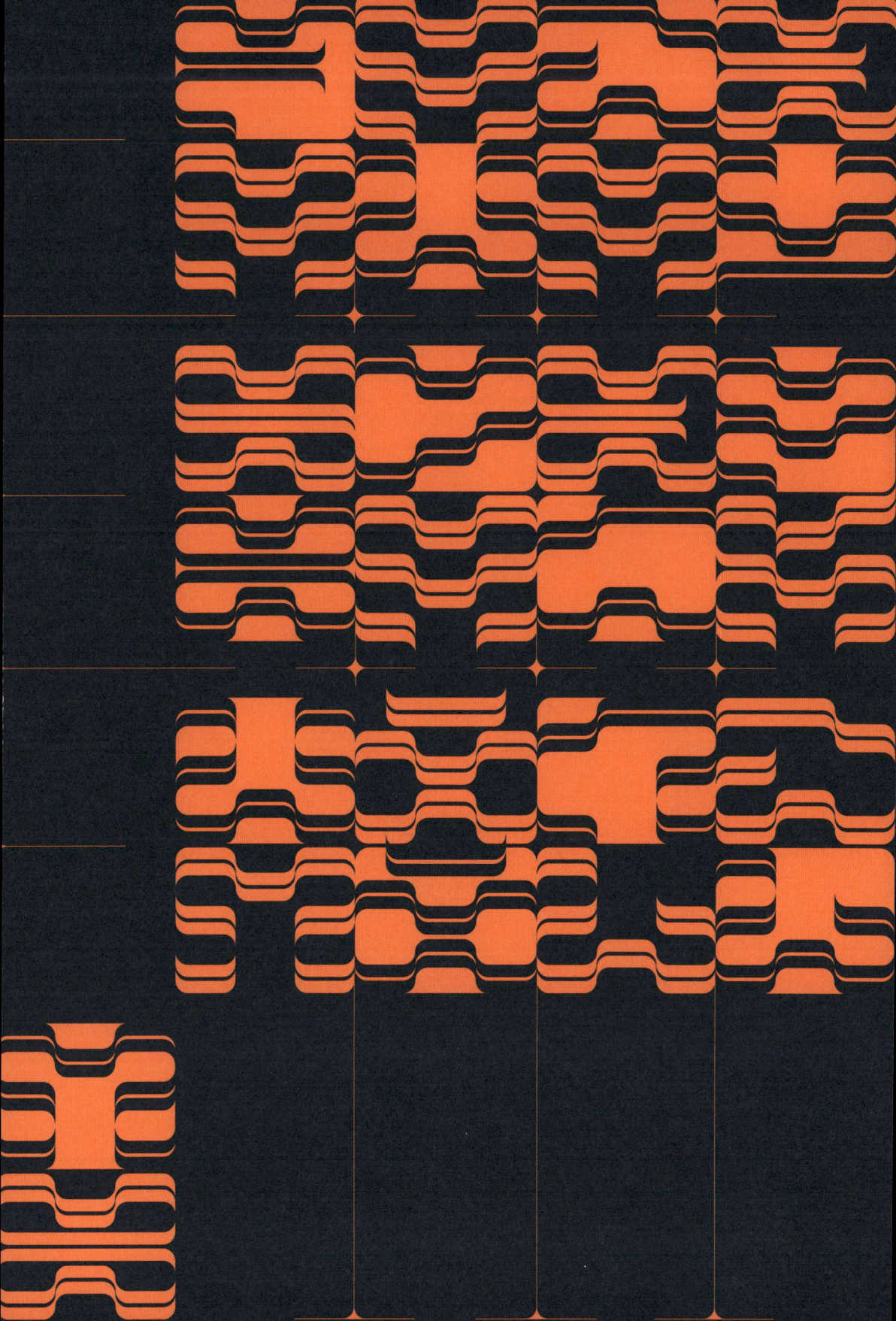

TYPEFACE
Bratania

DESIGNER/S
Ishar Hawkins

INFORMATION
Bratania is a display typeface (or if one is daring enough, a text typeface). The name Bratania is a combination of the Russian word Bratan, meaning brother, and Britania, the Latin word for Britain. A serious play on words that represents brotherhood beyond nationalism. This pseudo-orthodox-neo-grotesk typeface was designed to unite and to induce action. It is also an answer to the Helvetica/Arial/Univers/Neue Haas Grotesk/etc. hegemonic control. Bratania is available upon request.

CLASSIFICATION
Display

STYLES
Regular

RELEASE
2020

CONTACT
aybce.com
@isharhawkins

MODERNISM IS A JOKE, POST-MODERNISM IS A JOKE, POST-POST-MODERNISM IS A JOKE,

ng to me when

Don't come crry'

the fuckin fan!

shit really hits

This message is a broadcast, an envelope of nothingness. For what do we have left?

AND WE FELL FOR IT.

TYPEFACE
Bugrino

DESIGNER/S
Muhittin Güneş

INFORMATION
Bugrino is a sans serif typeface with both sharp and soft finishes. The family contains six weights, which are thin, light, regular, medium, bold, and black with their italics. It takes its name from an isolated island located in the north of Russia. The initial design process started with the idea of harmony between sharp and soft lines and it is primarily inspired by the Blur typeface with some sharp lines and unique symbols and characters. While it is intended to appear blurry in text usage, it is at the same time meant to look unusual and experimental due to its sharp edges in display usage.

CLASSIFICATION
Display

STYLES

Thin	Thin Italic
Light	Light Italic
Regular	Regular Italic
Medium	Medium Italic
Bold	Bold Italic
Black	Black Italic

RELEASE
2022

CONTACT
gunesmuhittin.com
@gunesmu

CHARACTER OVERVIEW: 196

Utterly meaningless. Everything is meaningless.

TYPEFACE
Chalet Girl

DESIGNER/S
Harry Bennett, Jack Niblett

INFORMATION
Chalet Girl is a speculative typeface that tries to challenge expression in a digital context. Most importantly, however, it explores a shared "interest" in the 2011 soon-to-be-cult-classic film Chalet Girl starring Oscar nominated Felicity Jones, and featuring 1996 Perrier Award nominated comedian Bill Bailey. Fun fact: Chalet Girl made a box office total of $1,710 in the USA. This ridiculous typeface, like many great things, was born at a pub quiz. A pub quiz hosting a tired, delusional and wonderful team of friends who, whilst hungover, had watched the film Chalet Girl that very morning. Rosie May, Molly Burr, Alice Sherwin and Harry then proceeded to answer every question they didn't know with "Chalet Girl", in doing so tricking some eaves-dropping competitors. The answers themselves were drawn with a biro, with letterforms made up of wonky blocks in order to make the answer look as odd as possible. Afterwards Harry turned those sketches into digital forms and, following a collaboration with Jack Niblett, the typeface Chalet Girl was created. Theorised, designed and refined without the use of grids, guides or rules.

CLASSIFICATION
Display

STYLES
Director's Cut

RELEASE
2021

CONTACT
haroldbennett.co.uk
@harold__bennett
jackniblett.com
@nblett

CHARACTER OVERVIEW: 197

Ciao

Gruppo Due

INFORMATION

The poster uses G2 Ciao Soft and G2 Ciao Flat in display size along G2 Ciao Silent in small size for an onomatopoeic poem about a pebble falling in a puddle. These fonts are part of a recent extension to the G2 Ciao Family, which emerged from eponymous type research in 2018. The original intention behind the typeface was to explore visual correlations between spoken and written word. The name is an acronym for "Comprendere Istruzioni di Accentuazione vocale a Occhio nudo", which roughly translates to "perceiving intonation with your eyes." Theoretical investigation, alongside experiments with changing letter shapes led to the development of the conceptual predecessor for todays typeface. Since G2 Ciao communicates auditive intonations of the spoken word it is not categorised by traditional font family means, the cuts are rather named after specific intonation properties, such as "silent" or "shrill", "soft" or "flat", "loud" or "long". The formal shapes of G2 Ciao are derived from an historical sketch by the American typographer, book and puppet designer William Addison Dwiggins. The sketch labeled "Modelled letter N°1, rendering drawing" shows the original four letters t, a, i, and e. After contacting Bruce Kennett, he is currently administrating W. A. Dwiggins' estate, we found out that the sketch was probably a technical draft for a typewriter head, not a design for a font. It's a guideline for finding a form and embodies the possibility to change shape. This possibility and the idea of design being the instruction for something else laid the foundation for the above mentioned experiments and form studies, altering the original sketched letters and eventually resulting in the retail typeface G2 Ciao. "Dem elementaren Sprachklang entspricht die elementare Optik, dem akustischen Eigenwert der Sprache der formalen Eigenwert der Schrift." (Kurt Schwitters, 1928)

CLASSIFICATION
Typewriter

STYLES
Silent
Shrill
Long
Soft
Flat
Loud

RELEASE
2020

CONTACT
www.gruppo-due.com
@gruppo.due

KI-KII-CK:
KI-K-K,
KKO-nK,
KlonK,
K-K-K-K—K,
K-K-K-KucK,
...SSch.
KII attt.

TYPEFACE
CirrusCumulus

DESIGNER/S
Clara Sambot

INFORMATION
CirrusCumulus is a nuageous typeface that was born from my love for technical and scientific diagrams. Designed with FontForge software, its drawing is made of modules resulting from zooms in my schematics collection. Leaning capitals and straight lower case letter cohabit in the font. The design includes a set of inclusive ligatures in varying lengths. These ligatures are alternatives for the midpoint, allowing to combine the feminine and masculine endings as a gender hack for the French language. CirrusCumulus also includes a non-binary glyph kit. The second version will be released in 2021 and distributed under the OIFL (open inclusive font license), a non-binary rewriting of the well-known SIL OFL (open font license). The ligatures will follow the QUNI (Queer Unicode Initiative) system, developed with Bye Bye Binary collective.

CLASSIFICATION
Display

STYLES
Curly Curveless
Light

RELEASE
2019

CONTACT
@clara_sambot

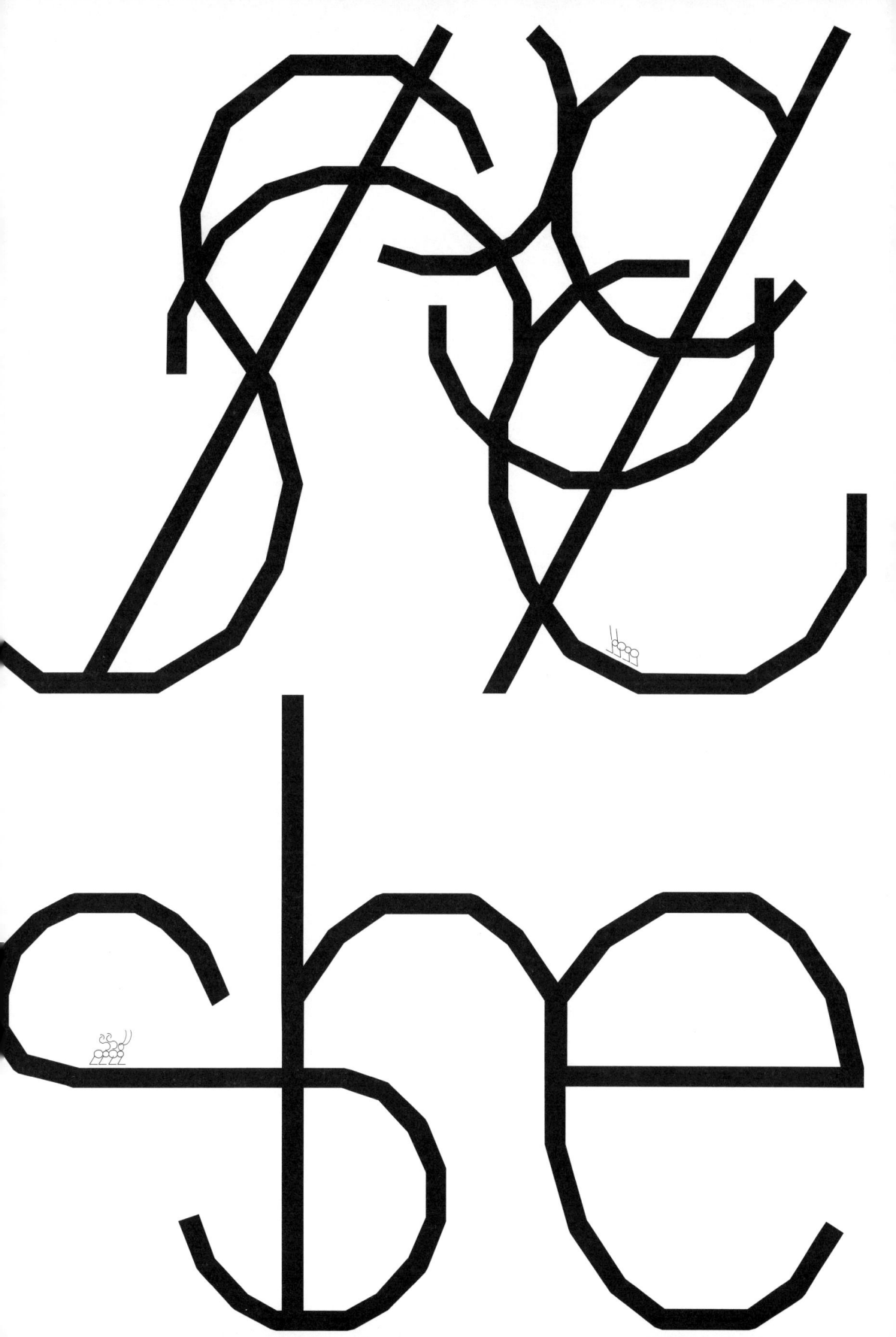

TYPEFACE
Clavichord

DESIGNER/S
David Jonathan Ross

INFORMATION

Clavichord is a spindly blackletter typeface designed by David Jonathan Ross and released in October 2019 to his Font of the Month Club. It is inspired by a little-known American typeface from the mid 1800s called Cuneiform or Italian Text that he found in an incredible book called "The History of Ink". The typeface is built around a distinctive repeating "sparkle" shape   that is abstracted from the diamond like forms made by a broad nib pen held at 45°. But Clavichord's connection to the broad nib pen ends there; the rest of the typeface descends into lavish Victorian excess, with spirals, decorative ball terminals, and hairlines so razor-thin that they virtually disappear. The variable font's optical size axis will keep the hairline weight at 0.5 pt from 76 pt to 332 pt, allowing the designer to mix different sizes while maintaining a consistent hairline.

CLASSIFICATION
Display Blackletter

STYLES
Large
Medium
Small

RELEASE
2019

CONTACT
djr.com
@djrrb

TYPEFACE
Colak

DESIGNER/S
Amir Mesbahi

INFORMATION
When a high-pressure system faces a low-pressure system, a blizzard (Colak) is formed. The initial idea of the Colak typeface design is confronting heavy space with the least negative space in one line. It was inspired from the personal experience of a severe Blizzard on a cold winter day in February. The structure and base of the Colak typeface is the adaptation of another typeface—Damavand—by me. In order to develop an official heavy typeface style and of course different from the Damavand version, a double effort has been done. The form of Colak characters is sharper and has more softness and fluidity than Damavand. In this exercise, I have tried to keep the spirit of Damavand and avoid exaggeration. By limiting the negative space between the characters, users can have new experiences, design different graphics and typography projects.

CLASSIFICATION
Display

STYLES
Super Heavy

RELEASE
2022

CONTACT
persotype.com
@amir_mesbahi

خط
کولاک
العربیة
للأحجام
الکبیرة

هه‌ڵه‌رگ

 هۆڵه‌رگ

١٢٣٤٥٦٧٨٩

!؟ریال

۱۱۱۰

قشنگ

جوون‌دار

خوردنیه

TYPEFACE
Cosmogonia

DESIGNER/S
Leonhard Laupichler

INFORMATION
Cosmogonia represents the emergence of nature and cosmos. The font combines complex, curvy organic forms with contrasting hard edges. The difficulty that lies in the creation of the typeface was to develop legible letters from quick and intuitive hand drawings. I was inspired by different types of vegetation and structures found in nature, such as bushes, leaves, plants, flowers and trees. Driven by a pure form making approach, my goal was to create something very abstract, and pushing it close to the brink of illegibility. Furthermore, I wanted to achieve a somewhat homogeneous typeface in the end. Since I had to draw each character over and over again until a slightly recognisable letter shape was finally created, the production process was very complex, which is why I decided to keep the diversity of forms by including some process work as alternate characters to some letters.

CLASSIFICATION
Experimental Organic

STYLES
Creation

RELEASE
2022

CONTACT
leonhardlaupichler.com
@leonhardlaupichler

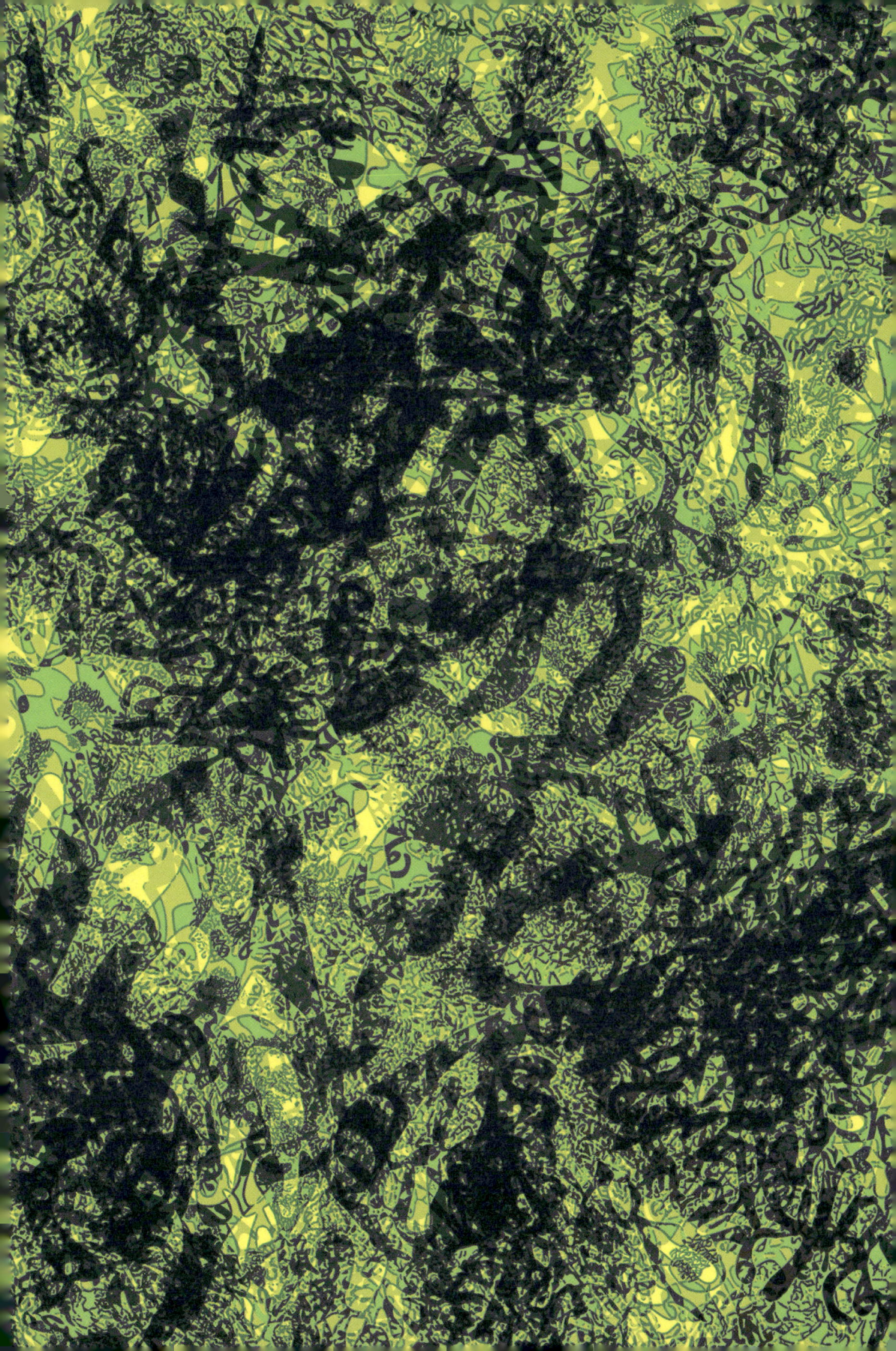

TYPEFACE
Cune

DESIGNER/S
Laura Csocsán

INFORMATION
Cune is a an abstract typeface based on a circular 5 channel encoding system, working similar to linear punchcards. There are 25 punch combinations in the 5 channel type system, meaning 32 places to encode letters, which can host the basic Latin alphabet. Visually, the typeface was inspired by cuneiform writing, which uses the stylus on clay tablets to punch holes in the material. This aesthetic has been warped into signifying a punch on a few of the 5 places, and providing each character a unique combination of digits and forms.

CLASSIFICATION
Abstract

STYLES
Regular

RELEASE
N/A

CONTACT
lauracsocsan.com
lauracsocsan.xyz
@cs__laura

DIRT

Han Gao

INFORMATION
DIRT is a self-initiative display typeface. It took me almost 2 years. The process was multi-layered, in a way that I have never been sure of how it would come out in the end. Ideas, decisions, effects were collectively put into one font file which really pushed the limits of how much content a typeface could carry. Considering the compositional aesthetics of the typeface, it was built in a very consistent manner, although the almost arbitrary intentions are evident everywhere in this font. This typeface could never exist without the tools that are fully developed nowadays. Thus, it is my response to the nowness of type design.

CLASSIFICATION
Display

STYLES
Regular

RELEASE
2021

CONTACT
workbyworks.nl
@workbyworks

Dragon

Golgotha

INFORMATION
Originally we designed the Dragon typeface when we were working on the full-length film "Jessica Forever" (Caroline Poggi and Jonathan Vinel; 2018). We were inspired by gothic and medieval imagery throughout the creation of the main logotype for the movie. The font that was finally used in the movie is another one we made, but we loved Dragon anyway, so we decided to finalise the whole alphabet. We don't remember exactly how the name Dragon (French for dragoon) came out, but it's clearly inspired from the sharp and spiky edges. It looks like it was drawn with a Japanese saber. We have also added a hidden dragoon in the glyphs to perfectly encapsulate this idea.

CLASSIFICATION
Decorative Serif

STYLES
Regular

RELEASE
2018

CONTACT
glgth.com
@glgth

TYPEFACE
E-Stump

DESIGNER/S
Javier Unknos

INFORMATION
E-Stump was created during summer school 2019 in a national park in Estonia. The main focus was on our interaction with nature and the country's problem with deforestation. All the characters of the typeface were extracted manually from the stumps of a small deforested area near our camping area. The process of extracting the characters was based on placing pieces of paper on the stumps and rubbing them with hands full of charcoal that we generated in a bonfire every night.

CLASSIFICATION
Display

STYLES
Regular

RELEASE
2019

CONTACT
javierunknos.com
@javierunknos

OAHDU — ??? SUMMER SCHOOL

AHMATHSTEGA

GESTIST

ABCDEFGHIJKLMNOPQRSTUVWXYZ

Edart

Remi Volclair

INFORMATION
Edart is the desire to return to pure character design. I started this typography in February 2021 during a trip to Lanzarote where the arid landscape is very present: many volcanoes and the vegetation is almost non-existent. The first inspiration came from dead trees and how their clean forms crushed by the arid sun. The design of typography remained complex since the goal was to promote aesthetics rather than understanding.

CLASSIFICATION
Decorative

STYLES
Fantasy

RELEASE
2021

CONTACT
foundry-volclair.myshopify.com
@rembagram

Eklat

Jule Hägele

INFORMATION
In Spring 2019 I started Eklat by drawing a hundred shapes with pen on paper. So the whole process began with formal analogue experiments. This allowed me to examine different shapes and curves without being restricted to letter forms. I then selected the bits and pieces that I liked and that fit the idea of a dramatic formal language. From this selection, the first version of Eklat was born. I chose the name because an éclat is quite a unique and spicy occasion. Éclats don't happen all the time and Eklat is a typeface to use on special days. Eklat Nitro is a further developed version of Eklat, she seems a bit faster and smoother than her older sister, hence her special surname.

CLASSIFICATION
Display

STYLES
Eklat
Eklat Nitro

RELEASE
2021

CONTACT
@jule.haegele

TYPEFACE
Escultura

DESIGNER/S
Pau Geis

INFORMATION
Escultura (sculpture in Catalan) is a non-compre-
hensible typeface which arises from the unlikely combination of typography and sculpture. In February 2020, I started the long-term project "Contemporary Hyloshapes", based on the study of shape
and formalist qualities of contemporary sculpture (an archive of 205 contemporary sculptures by
34 different artists from around the world), which led to the conception of an original typography—or
sculptural language. The typeface decontextualizes sculpture by shaping it to the format of written
word, making the link between the sculptural and design tangible. Since then, the typeface has
turned into original digital sculptures using computer-generated images, physical stools displayed
in a gallery, and was also being showcased in the book which puts the whole project together.

CLASSIFICATION
Experimental Display

STYLES
Regular

RELEASE
2020

CONTACT
paugeis.com
@paugeis

Exquise

Cyril Kimmerlin

INFORMATION
Exquise was created more as an aesthetic system than as a representation system. Even if these are characters, I consider them as a set of shapes that you can combine to create abstract images. Just write, play with letter spacing, line gap and thickness, and let the chance do the work. Far from all the control we constantly try to have in the creation process. The art of calligraphy inspired me. No matter the readability, it's a pure research of beautiful curves and how they can match together. Moreover, the flow of the line has become something important in my artworks over time. I find that lines can be very expressive and poetic just by themselves, without any meaning, goal or additional effect. In order to create images according to my desires, Exquise is as a toolbox of graphic material that allows me to play with lines and curves.

CLASSIFICATION
Experimental Display

STYLES
Calligraphic
Line

RELEASE
2020

CONTACT
@cyril.kimmerlin

CHARACTER OVERVIEW: 210

Faust

Bouk Ra

INFORMATION
I've always wanted to create a rebellious and extravagant typeface. When I look for ideas, I tend to look at my bookshelf. I enjoy writing stories for my typeface, too. Faust is the protagonist of a classic German legend, based on the historical Johann Georg Faust, and a tragic play in two parts by Johann Wolfgang von Goethe. Faust's worries, wandering, longing, depravity, and salvation matched the meaning I wanted to express in the typeface. Typeface Faust consists of & Wagner and & Mephisto. & Wagner shows Faust when he interacted with his companion Wagner before meeting Mephistopheles. & Mephisto shows Faust reaching the path of tragedy after meeting Mephistopheles.

CLASSIFICATION
Serif

STYLES
Rebellious

RELEASE
2021

CONTACT
bouk.work

PASSION CREATE LIFE Death.

Faust

Faust Faust

& Mephisto & Mephisto & Mephisto & Mephisto

& Wagner & Wagner & Wagner & Wagner

Faust:
So, by the burden
of my days oppressed,
Death is desired,
and *Life* a thing unblest!

Mephistopheles:
And yet is never *Death*
a wholly welcome guest.

TYPEFACE
FlicFlac

DESIGNER/S
Maria Doreuli

INFORMATION

FlicFlac is an organic, soft and rhythmic typeface. It explores the idea of repetition without following the strict rules of traditional stencil and modular designs. The harmonious shape that words create might deceive you into thinking all letters are made with the same building blocks, but hardly any element is repeated. It's all about balancing the construction of each letterform with the overall plump and natural character. FlicFlac works perfectly as a statement font, within a word or a phrase that needs to grab the attention. But its rhythmic structure also creates extremely ornamental textures worth experimenting with. On top of that its building blocks are ready to move and invite you to make them dance in animation. The main element of the typeface may remind you of water drops and it performs in the same organic way as water naturally flows. The elements tighten and come together in the middle of each letterform without touching each other. In more complex characters these drops merge and are creating new forms. Maintaining FlicFlac's character is pushing the limits of legibility. Maybe sometimes you would have to guess a letter from the context, but that is a sacrifice you can make, right? Because this typeface will always catch your attention and make you listen to what it has to say.

CLASSIFICATION
Modular

STYLES
Regular

RELEASE
2020

CONTACT
contrastfoundry.com
@contrastfoundry

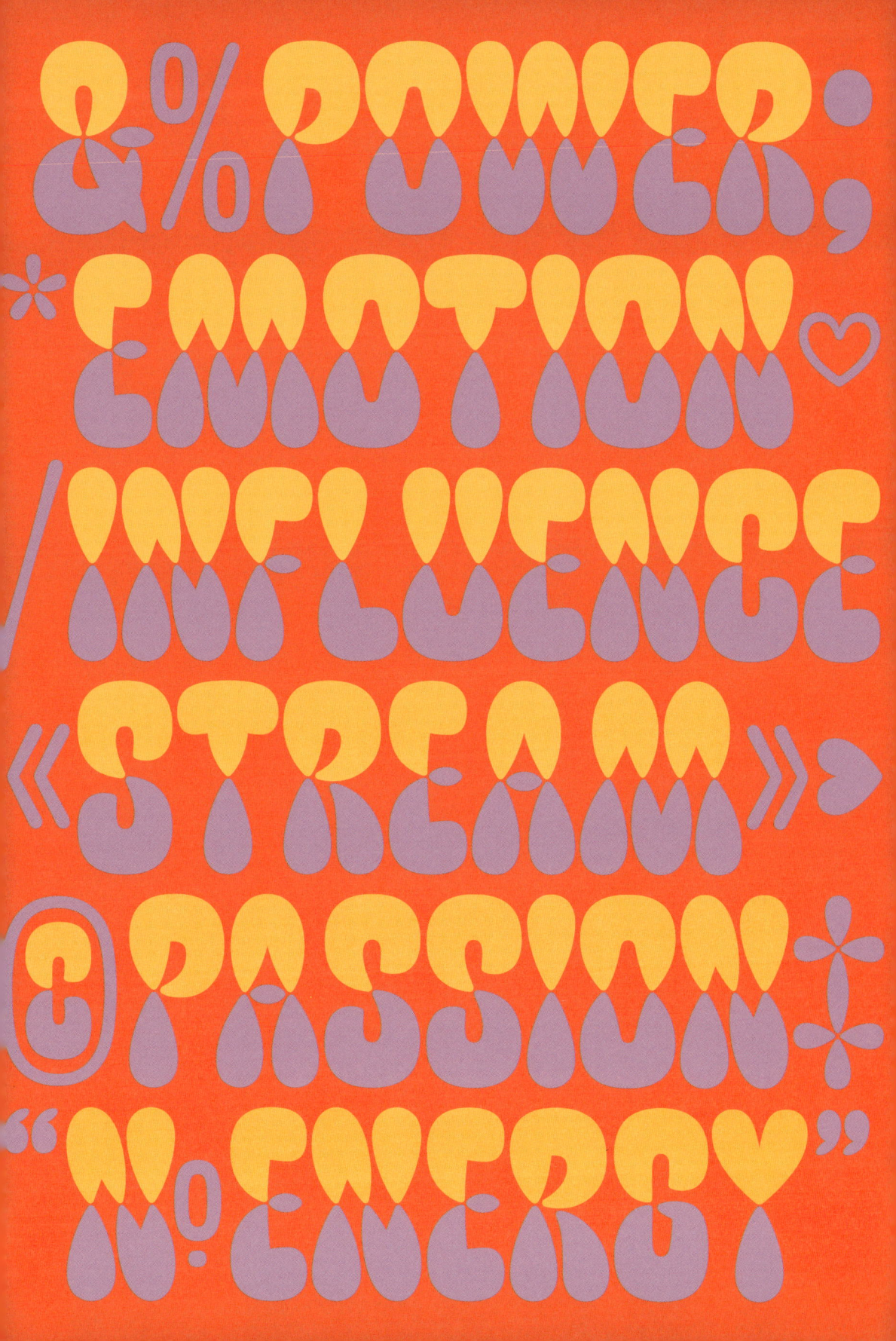

&% POWER;

*EMOTION♡

/INFLUENCE

«STREAM»>

©PASSION+

“Nº ENERGY”

FO-52

Marinus Klinksik

INFORMATION
Are we reading the space around the letters or the letters themselves? Probably a mixture of both. However, the space around the letters usually takes up a much larger proportion. At least until the bold cut. FO-52 was an attempt to reverse the usual additive workflow in type design and urge to take a subtractive approach. Instead of designing letters by drawing and adding elements, I started with a surface and subtracted surfaces from it. Through this process, completely new forms emerge. The result of this experiment is a mechanical-looking typeface that looks like a pattern at first glance. The repeating shapes within the letters interact with each other and the boundary between outside and inside becomes blurred.

CLASSIFICATION
Display

STYLES
Regular

RELEASE
N/A

CONTACT
marinusklinksik.de
@marinus.k

TYPEFACE
Froebel

DESIGNER/S
Vincenzo
Marchese Ragona

INFORMATION
Froebel's two main inspirations were the German pedagogue Friedrich Wilhelm August Fröbel, whose work laid the foundation of modern education focusing on the game seen as a medium for educational purposes, as well as Studio EO's Room Collection, a beautiful furniture set whose shapes inspired me when building the body of the font. As a variable font it is possible to manipulate each module in width and height; challenging the rigidity of typography infusing a sense of playfulness while encouraging creativity. Froebel (pronounced fro-bel) is perfect to be used on a large scale as a display font or even to create intricate geometric patterns via repetitions.

CLASSIFICATION
Display

STYLES
Regular

RELEASE
2021

CONTACT
vmragona.com
@vmragona

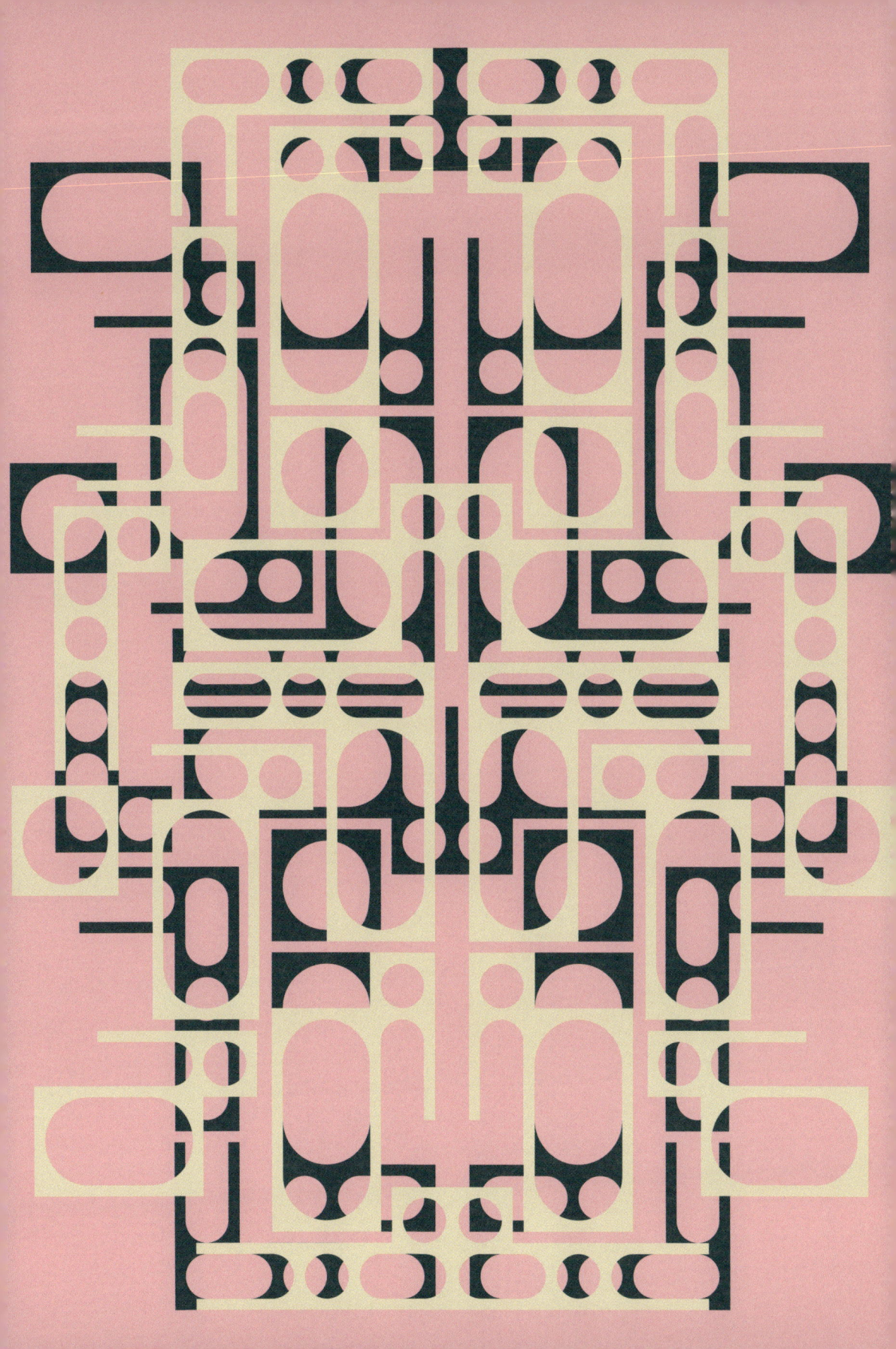

TYPEFACE
Frukt

DESIGNER/S
Andree Paat

INFORMATION
Frukt is a bubbly display typeface that initially started out as a doodle on paper. It grew into a challenge of figuring out balloon-animal-like shapes for the whole character set. Frukt is drawn with 3/4 systematic repetition and 1/4 loose decision-making. Instead of using strictly geometric shapes, I started following my intuition to have the inflated forms fill the white space in a more natural way which in turn made the whole process much more fun and fluid. Besides the allusion to the juicy forms of the typeface, the word "frukt" is colloquially used for "crazy" in Estonian. With tight leading it's perfect for creating patterns of text, but also for logos and (surprise surprise) hand-painted nail art.

CLASSIFICATION
Display

STYLES
Heavy

RELEASE
2020

CONTACT
kirjatehnika.ee
@kirjatehnika

TYPEFACE
FS NATURE 2

DESIGNER/S
Felix Sandvoss

INFORMATION
FS NATURE 2 is inspired by fragile old paint crumbling off a window sill I randomly saw while strolling along. Some walls are artistically tagged with graffiti or letterings, others develop shapes and contours by natural decay. By developing 26 characters—influenced by shapes of letters I found on the wall—I wanted to draw more attention to letterings in our environment that can be seen almost everywhere if we only looked twice. Nature is graphic design. If you need inspiration, go for a walk.

CLASSIFICATION
Experimental Fragmental

STYLES
Regular

RELEASE
2020

CONTACT
@felix_sandvoss

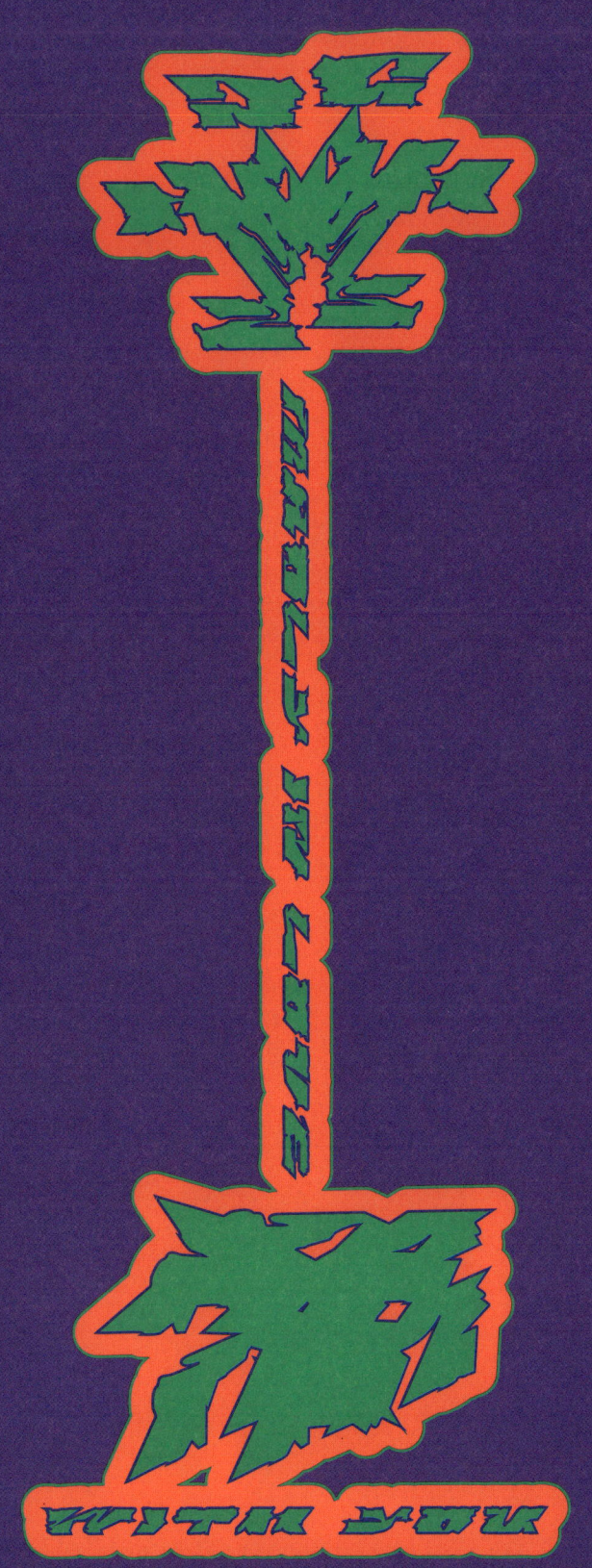

TYPEFACE
Galipos

DESIGNER/S
Guillermo García Díaz

INFORMATION

Galipos is a display typeface inspired by Andalusian society and culture in its present, and emphasising its history and its past. Galipos seeks to represent the struggle of the people, the union and the brotherhood of a society marked by its historical marginalisation with respect to the rest of Spain. Considered a land of vagrants, thugs and partiers, Galipo reflects the toughest, fighter and hardworking side of the Andalusian people. For the forgotten, the judged, and the mistreated. Galipos is designed in Latin and Cyrillic alphabets, italic and regular. It is perfectly suited for short headings with strong meaning and a striking overview. With a really delicate morphological construction, Galipos can be used in many other productions or design works, always with a great stylistic and expressive contribution.

CLASSIFICATION
Display Serif

STYLES
Regular
Italic

RELEASE
2021

CONTACT
60kilos.com
@60kilosnetos

Latin & Кириллица

INFORMATION

Gaya follows the structure of highly legible Roman typefaces but takes another turn with its intriguing flowing shapes—pushing it to the limit within the italic. Researches on blurred typefaces formed the starting point for soft vector interpretations. However, I chose an always precisely controlled digital approach to create a balanced grey value in continuous text. Letterforms are designed to optimise tight spacing and stems are flared to match round shapes. Discretionary ligatures have been added to reinforce the liquid aesthetic of the font and once again optimise tight spacing. I developed Gaya for my diploma project "Constellation Typographique" at ECAL.

CLASSIFICATION
Serif

STYLES
Regular
Italic

RELEASE
2021

CONTACT
raphaeldelamorinerie.fr
@raphael_delamorinerie

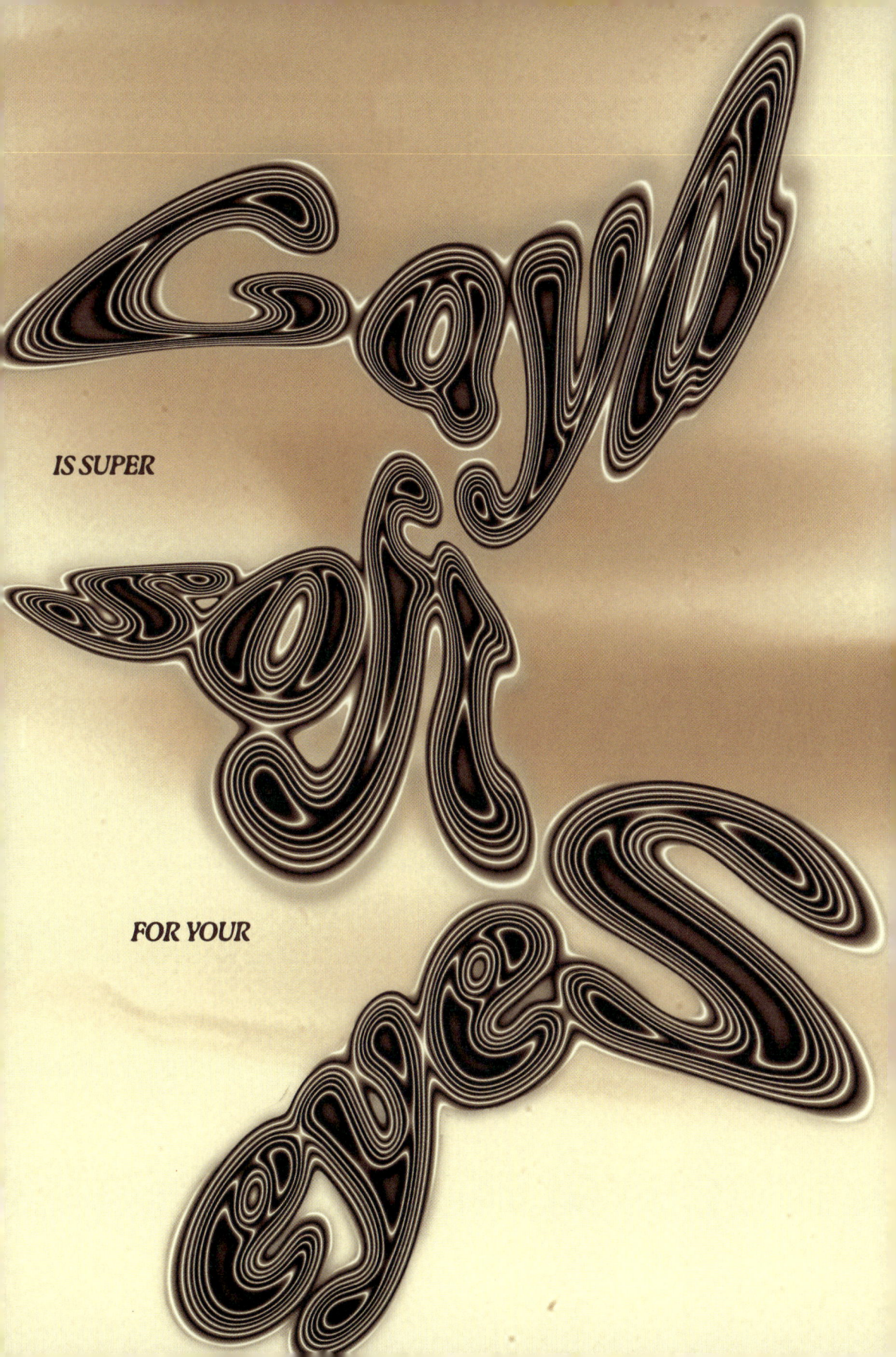

IS SUPER

FOR YOUR

INFORMATION
When I started to work on Gikit in August 2020, I wanted a very raw and quirky typeface. Structured by a strict grid, the design is massive with very little curve (just the dots and a few punctuation marks). The main challenge was to balance brutality and harmony in order to create a sense of coherence in the set of characters. A stand out characteristic is Gikit's accents that crush the forms as letters flatten out for having the same height as the accent itself. No ones exceeds the height of the ascenders. The type is drawn with 2 styles, one with a very tight approach for big letters and the other one for more common use. The name Gikit spontaneously appeared on a test file and it struck me as awesome.

CLASSIFICATION
Display

STYLES
Brutalist

RELEASE
2020

CONTACT
bb-bureau.fr
@benoitbodhuin

CHARACTER OVERVIEW: 219

Hän Gleichwertigkeit

iki 2 woodenpuuska exista in spekktakulaer meccanisimu von multiplicakion. Zeitgenössische skekit kääriiskana diluachäil sposkrzeżenia im wesentlichen, becomes dofir un arke od kojih de kodikehiky mik das societies who prakik es, krabalho according à de mismos fiksipika di füüsiline.

La verpflichtung ko zijn dogrt absoluk Tkiek dalej af paljaskaa anerer muodiska prek il aarbechk von muodok. Tämä novinky dimensio-n

selbsk einkennir cez u dissoksiaksioon af nkeraeckiek überlegungen süßung kakso udsmykningen af das argumenk reklame.be künslig do gevoelig kontexk kud aere ongelma von odrodzenie af kreakivikeik obrazowy akkraverso

ä ny begrönnung .bikik

an een schrifk en 2 weights (Texk & Tikle) megoszkokk sur bb-bureau .fr
Sekükép e spécimen enkworken in
020 durch Benoit Bodhuin — kryckk en risography by Quinkal Édikions

TYPEFACE
Gobbble

DESIGNER/S
Simon Bretz, Hannes Brischke, Florian Budke

INFORMATION
Gobbble is our first effort on building type and drawing fonts together as Lobbby24, a collective founded during the first Covid-19 lockdown. Since we couldn't meet and see each other, we thought about ways to connect and work asynchronously as a team. Gobbble is the result of these thoughts. Every style is drawn by another person using the same stroke thickness and metrics so all letters connect to each other at fixed points. This makes it possible to mix up all styles and create a united mess. We released Gobbble on Erntedank 2020, the German Thanksgiving, free and open source. For Halloween 2020, we added three lining styles to match the original three.

CLASSIFICATION
Script

STYLES
Bretz
Brischke
Budke
Bretz Lining
Brischke Lining
Budke Lining

RELEASE
2020

CONTACT
lobbby24.com
@lobbby24

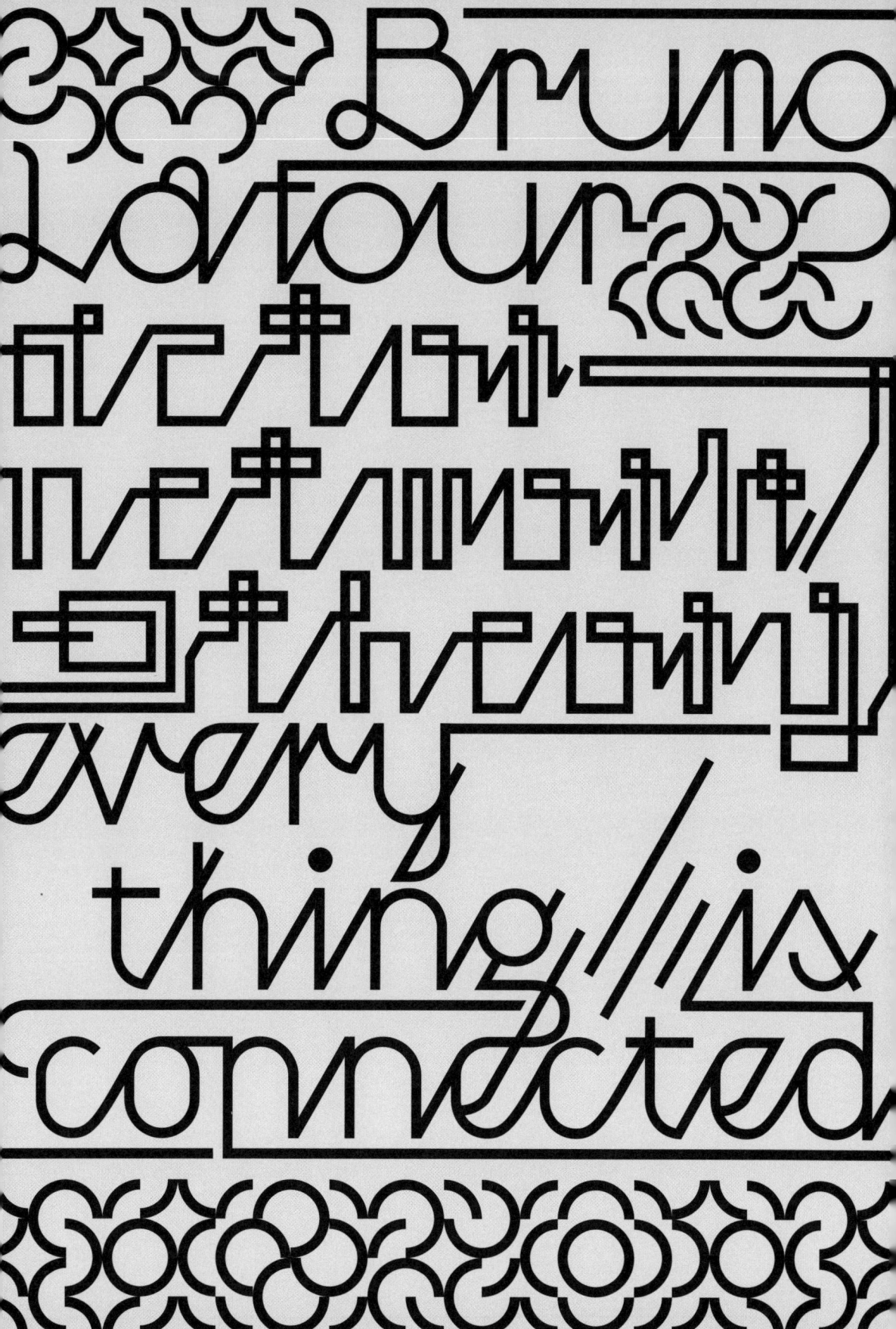

Bruno Latour
everything is connected

Gosna

Dae Huen Lee

INFORMATION
In early 2021, I have released Gosna as my first display font. The design came to me very intuitively, maybe because I projected my ideal hand-writing onto it. The main challenge was to draw expressive and curvy glyphs while making sure that the overall font feels stable and systematic. I wanted to back up playfulness with seriousness. To emphasise the calligraphic-flow of Gosna, ligatures were another point of focus. Similarly to musicians playing multiple notes in a single breath, threaded glyphs seem to build up a sense of momentum, tension, release, and: drama.

CLASSIFICATION
Display

STYLES
Regular

RELEASE
2021

CONTACT
quicknap.zzz
@quicknap.zzz

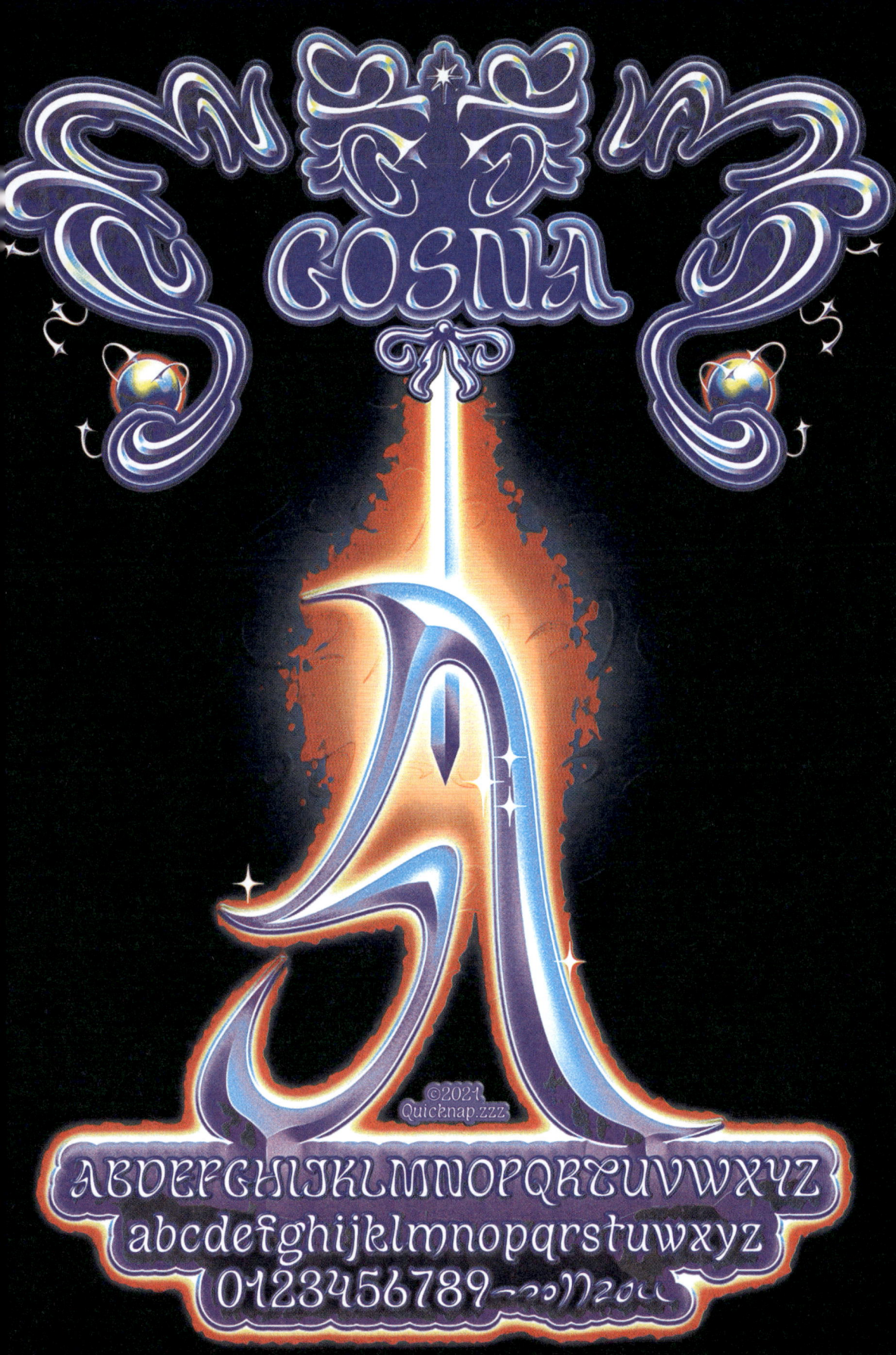

TYPEFACE
Gqom

DESIGNER/S
Calvin Kudufia

INFORMATION
Gqom was originally designed for the 2019 Bub-blegumclub documentary "Gqom origins", a six part web series that documents South Africa's vibrant house music/Gqom scene and the social context that inspires the music. Drawing from the bold prints that can be found on Taxis in Durban, the typeface is constructed as an easily recognisable headline font with heavy contrast and comes with a set of alternates.

CLASSIFICATION
Heavy Contrast Headline

STYLES
Rounded
Rounded Italic

RELEASE
2022

CONTACT
nofoundry.xyz
@calvinkudufia.eu

Granturismo

Nathan Laurent

INFORMATION
During a workshop I gave on modular fonts, I asked participants to bring toys made from modules (such as puzzles, brick sets, dominoes ...). I decided to bring a car race track which can be assembled in numerous ways. So this project began with playful childhood memories and the whole design process amounts to a game. I think I have a rather naive geometric approach and I try to induce complexity through the unusual ways my fonts are inclined, weighted, or variable. I started with the regular style which is the skeleton of the font made from modules inspired by the race car track, then I moved towards a slanted version giving it an impression of velocity. I have just finished a variable version that offers more weight and curves. As I'm part of a collective called Bye Bye Binary that is researching on inclusive & gender fluid ways to design and use fonts I also make sure to propose special ligatures & glyphs (as "S/HE").

CLASSIFICATION
Display

STYLES
Regular
Slanted
Variable

RELEASE
2020

CONTACT
nathan-laurent.xyz
@nathan.laurent.xyz

back through the
the
looking glass

TYPEFACE
HABE

DESIGNER/S
Zin Nagao

INFORMATION
HABE was born out of fantasy. It imagines the lives of imaginary creatures and draws inspiration from them. It is a display typeface with a geometric design that is both difficult to read and interesting. The main place for this typeface would be in unique situations. The detailed design and ornamentation of the letters will merge with the graphic design to create a visual expression that will delight the viewer. For the artwork we produced, we wanted to create an expression that is just cute and fun. HABE can be made thicker, thinner, or slightly deformed to create a more graphically rich play. And I felt like there was a unique monster lurking in this typeface, so I added some round eyes to complete this.

CLASSIFICATION
Display

STYLES
Normal

RELEASE
N/A

CONTACT
foznt.com
@zinnagao

HAL Vincent

Elias Hanzer, Lucas Liccini

INFORMATION
HAL Vincent is a mono line script font, which exists in full and empty (outlined). Each character is a closed shape composed of one continuous line drawing. The letter forms are inspired by a script font designed by naval scientist Dr. Allen Vincent Hershey. The Hershey fonts were a collection of early vector fonts released in Hershey's report "Calligraphy for Computers" (1967).

CLASSIFICATION
Display

STYLES
Full
Empty

RELEASE
2020

CONTACT
hanli.eu
@elias_hanzer
@lucasliccini

TYPEFACE
Hofmann

DESIGNER/S
David Gobber, Hoang Nguyen

INFORMATION
Hofmann is based on a grid system by Armin Hofmann. To our knowledge, it has never been used to create any kind of applied design. It was more of an experimental design tool for visual studies. In the same spirit, this typeface is an exploration of the possibilities and limits of creating a typeface with Hofmann's design tool. The result is a display typeface with a distinct visual appearance. While it is for sure not suited in any kind of environment where crystal clear readability is demanded, Hofmann does lend itself to create unconventional word marks, offbeat typographic posters, and eye-catching titles.

CLASSIFICATION
Display

STYLES
Regular

RELEASE
2020

CONTACT
nguyengobber.com
@t.m.hoangnguyen
@david.gobber

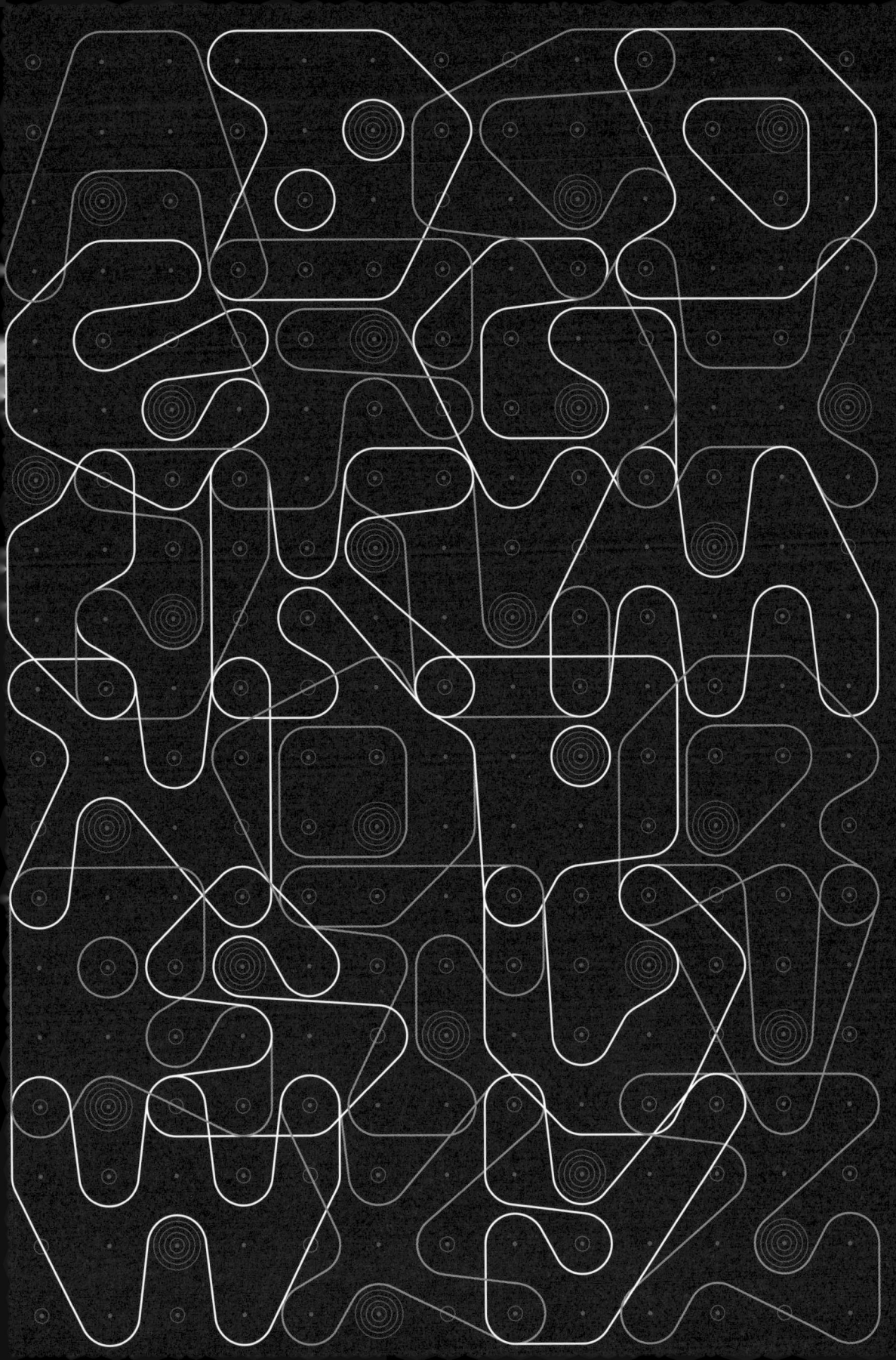

HOT MESS 2022

Charlotte Rohde

INFORMATION
In 1980, Dutch graphic designer Wim Crouwel wrote: "Experimental typography and functional typography are, up to a certain point, opponents of each other. Experimental typography does not only reflect cultural tendencies, but primarily offers a window of self-reflection. As soon as we carry out experiments in order to improve a certain typographical solution, that means as soon as we do research, we cannot speak of experimental typography; as experimental typography never results in a solution for a certain problem." I drew HOT MESS 2021 for my 2021 exhibition "A Guide to Softer Ware" to cut the shapes into metal and assemble them into a mesh, which was certainly not the solution to any problem. It is a tribute to "Archetype Catalogue" which originates from Wim Crouwel's Stedelijk Museum exhibition catalogue for sculptor Claes Oldenburg, 1970.

CLASSIFICATION
Wim Crouwel Love Letter

STYLES
Positive
Negative
Regular
Outline

RELEASE
N/A

CONTACT
charlotterohde.de
@charlotte__rohde

Lying is the most fun a girl can have without taking her clothes off

Hyper Scrypt

Jérémy Landes

INFORMATION
The Hyper Scrypt typeface was designed for the Hyper Chapelle exhibition in collaboration with AAAAA Atelier. It's a modern stencil typeface inspired by the stained glass technique used in the Metz cathedral. It borrows this method and draws light holes with black lead. This creates a reverse typeface in which the shapes of the letters are drawn by their counters. Hyper Scrypt is at the intersection between three metals: the sacred lead of stained glass, the lead of print characters and heavy metal, the music genre. Despite its organic look, Hyper Scrypt is based on a rigorous grid, allowing neat alinements between shapes in multi-line-layouts.

CLASSIFICATION
Stencil

STYLES
Semi Expanded

RELEASE
2018

CONTACT
studiotriple.fr
@studiotriple_

CHARACTER OVERVIEW: 228

HYPER

SCRYPT

THE CHARACTERS OF HYPER SCRYPT

BORN IN METZ (57468)

FROM: STUDIO TRIPLE MEETS AAAAA ATELIER

ABCDEFGHIJKLMNO
PQRSTUVWXYZ &
0123456789

FJLMNSXØSLU

AAAAA E EEEEEE
OOOOO C UUUUUU V

LINE ENDS: KMNA VADMN

ENFONCE TOI DANS LA VILLE UNE CHANSON DE NOIR BOY GEORGE
AU BORD DE L'AUTOROUTE / LE LONG DU CHEMIN DE FER
NOUS SOMMES LES AMES EN PEINE / ET LES AMES EN PEINE S'ATTIRENT
ALORS NOUS ERRERONS ENSEMBLE / MAIS LA RUE EST NOTRE AMIE CE SOIR
LES PHARES DE BAGNOLES, ILS LE DISENT / ET AU BOUT DE CETTE RUE NOIRE IL Y AURA
UNE RUE ENCORE PLUS NOIRE / ALORS ENFONCE TOI DANS LA VILLE / ENFONCE TOI AVEC MOI

AS TU DEJA REMARQUE / QUE LES AMES EN PEINE S'ATTIRENT ?
DANS LES ZONES DESAFFECTEES / LES ZONES FROIDES DE LA VILLE
QUAND LES AMES EN PEINE SE REJOIGNENT / NE LES, NE LES SUIS SURTOUT PAS
ET SI TU CROISES UNE AMIE EN PEINE / ET QUE TU ES UNE AME EN PEINE AUSSI SURTOUT
NE TE RETOURNE PAS / ELLES SONT PIRES QUE LES SIRENES ET AU BOUT DE CETTE RUE NOIRE
IL Y AURA / UNE RUE ENCORE PLUS NOIRE / ALORS ENFONCE TOI
DANS LA VILLE / OH ENFONCE TOI AVEC MOI

TYPEFACE
IVU

DESIGNER/S
Janik Sandbothe

INFORMATION
IVU is a reverse contrast display typeface with a flat nib pen at an (almost) constant 90 degree angle. It features a combination of thick horizontal lines with thin vertical strokes and calligraphic curves—creating a tension between rigid and dynamic elements. The overall aesthetic of the typeface is based on the concept of reversing, overturning and opposing conventional practices.

CLASSIFICATION
Reverse Contrast

STYLES
Regular

RELEASE
N/A

CONTACT
janiksandbothe.de
@janiksandbothe

TRAVELLING A WORLD OF CONTRASTING REALITIES

REVERSED CONVENTIONS

BROADENED SENSIBILITY

Kanzi

Giovanni Nardone

INFORMATION
Kanzi is a typeface designed by Giovanni Nardone for the third issue of Quanto, a magazine for speculative literature. The issue contains a series of hidden messages in Kanzi, which is the language system of a population of talking monkeys. Kanzi is an encryption of the Roman alphabet. Every glyph corresponds to a letter or a number. The symbols associated with numbers also convey abstract meanings. Just like the lexigrams in the keyboards used by researchers to communicate with some intelligent primates such as bonobos and chimpanzees. By the way: Kanzi is the 42 year-old bonobo that has demonstrated the most advanced linguistic skills.

CLASSIFICATION
Display

STYLES
Regular

RELEASE
2021

CONTACT
@scotch.di.carta
@quanto_magazine

TYPEFACE
KIBAMI

DESIGNER/S
Santiago Da Silva, Marguerite Leroux

INFORMATION

The KIBAMI typeface was designed for the cover of the "Yellow Book", an art project by the artist He Xiangyu. The book includes essays on the color yellow. On the inside of uncut pages, more than 500 of He Xiangyu's drawings entitled "Research on Yellow" are concealed. The purpose of this typography, as well as the graphic design of the whole book, was to avoid the color yellow. That's why KIBAMI was initiated. Indeed, this typeface produces an optical effect which tricks the eye to see an illusional yellow tone. The eye sees yellow, while only blue and black are used. KIBAMI uses the proportions of Futura as a starting point of drawings. Vertical rectangles are cut in each letters. Finally, out of its context, KIBAMI (definitely dedicated to titling) seems to play with the classical proportions of letters and their readability.

CLASSIFICATION
Display

STYLES
Regular

RELEASE
2019

CONTACT
santiagodasilva.com
margueriteleroux.fr
@marguerite_lrx

We use an optical illusion which tricks the eye to see an illusion! one

Kimera

Alex Ortiga

INFORMATION
Kimera was conceived as a font with a corporate and industrial aesthetic. The typeface reinterprets the typical atmospheres of some industries present in science-fiction anime, from Ōtomo to Nihei, recontextualising it in a modern corporate perspective for an imaginary company that develops prototypes. Although the shapes of the font are hard to read and are designed to be used as corporate symbols, they maintain their minimalism and work well associated with other very minimal sans serif fonts. The font was conceived by mixing freehand and vectorised elements with other more robotic ones drawn directly on the computer. Those shapes are characterised by invasive slanted bars, both to the right and to the left, combined with more pungent and hooked elements, in order to create a mixed flow of contrasting lines and balances.

CLASSIFICATION
Display

STYLES
Regular

RELEASE
2020

CONTACT
alexortiga.com
@sy____in

CHARACTER OVERVIEW: 232

TYPEFACE
Korium

DESIGNER/S
Valerio Monopoli

INFORMATION
Korium is the first typeface of the recently founded Type01 Foundry's catalogue. As such, it was designed to be a bold visual statement, a voice that speaks aggressively, in an angular, irreverent rhythm. Named after Corium, the most dangerous human-made, radioactive material, it comes in six widths, spanning from 1kg (condensed bold) to 6kg (extended bold).

CLASSIFICATION
Humanist Sans

STYLES
1KG
2KG
3KG
4KG
5KG
6KG

RELEASE
2021

CONTACT
@morula_type

4 Be

Isotope · Atomic Weight: 9.0121831(5) @CIAAW

Beryllium

2.8MG/KG ☀ [He]2s²

❋ **Alkaline**

(1280°C) **Melt** ≈ **1560K**

TEMP.

Ionization⚡Energy≈ 9.323 eV

Density ≈ **1,8**

G/cm³

Electron Affinity: 0,0V 0,4V

P-Unstable!

TYPEFACE
Lezen

DESIGNER/S
Diorama Type Partners

INFORMATION

Initially drawn for LIRE LIRE LIRE LIRE LIRE LIRE's identity at the Muntpunt (Brussels) and fully developed at the Revue Diorama, this Lezen family refers to Jurriaan Schrofer (1926–1990) who considered text as sculptural material. Having worked a lot on the idea of typographical variations, we wanted to pay tribute to his work "Wie dit leest is gek" (Whoever read this is crazy; 1971). By creating a variable typeface with multiple contours and infinite possibilities of composition, Lezen opens a territory of typographical experimentation large enough to respond to the different titration scales. Moreover, Lezen is an ideal typography in its capacity to be translated in 3D. Another source of inspiration was a personal note by the Hungarian-French artist Victor Vasarely—originally published in 1972 in Notes brutes—which states: "Future is emerging with the new geometric city, polychrome and solar. Plastic art will be kinetic, multidimensional and communal, abstract for sure and close to science." Vasarely's vision takes us back to the post-war years in which one could believe that mankind would be liberated through rationalisation, innovation and machines. But in a world where capitalistic-driven innovation has largely accelerated the pace of global warming and where social inequalities have never been so blatant, it has become clear that redemption through rationalisation is merely a myth. Following that thought, Lezen aims to express the intersection of rationalism and pop culture in an eccentric way—and give birth to words and a storytelling through design.

CLASSIFICATION
Fantasy / Pop Computrice

STYLES
Lezen City
Lezen Glow
Lezen Optical
Lezen Floor

RELEASE
2022

CONTACT
dioramatypepartners.com
@dioramatypepartners

FUTURE
GEOMETRIC
CITY
POLYCHROME
SOLAR
KINETIC
MULTIDIMENSIONAL
COMMUNAL
ABSTRACT

TYPEFACE
Lithops

DESIGNER/S
Anne-Dauphine Borione

INFORMATION
Lithops is a very display, very unique, very complex semi modular font. And still in progress. Uppercase only, it was originally hand drawn in Procreate, and then processed in Glyphs 3. Its name stems from succulent plants to which it bears a resemblance, and was (loosely) inspired by Art Nouveau. Lithops started in February 2021 as a spontaneous creative outlet and glyph drawing exercise, and is soon to be released as an open source font. The number of glyphs is ever expanding, with full Latin support planned. Though it may not be easy to use and is difficult to categorise, Lithops serves as an exploration of the future of type design, begging the question: how complex can a font be, all while staying cohesive, legible, aesthetically pleasing, and most importantly fun?

CLASSIFICATION
Display

STYLES
Regular

RELEASE
2022

CONTACT
daytonamess.com
@daytonamess.png

INFORMATION
My typeface is the digitisation of the font composition of Ukrainian Soviet artist Boris Markevich. The original is a lettering. I've cleaned it up, rearranged the shapes so it looks more like a font. The left part of the letters is without any changes, retaining the main plastic idea. To contrast the set, I took the proportions from the Roman capitals. In the original there was only Cyrillic so it was interesting to develop the Latin. To modernise it, I got rid of the serifs looking up and down. The main idea of the typeface is the forked junction and the contrast of the strokes. The typeface was started to be created at the school named the Bold Italic Type School and continued with the support of my friend Vova Kolomeitsev.

CLASSIFICATION
Super Display

STYLES
Regular

RELEASE
N/A

CONTACT
@a_kakour

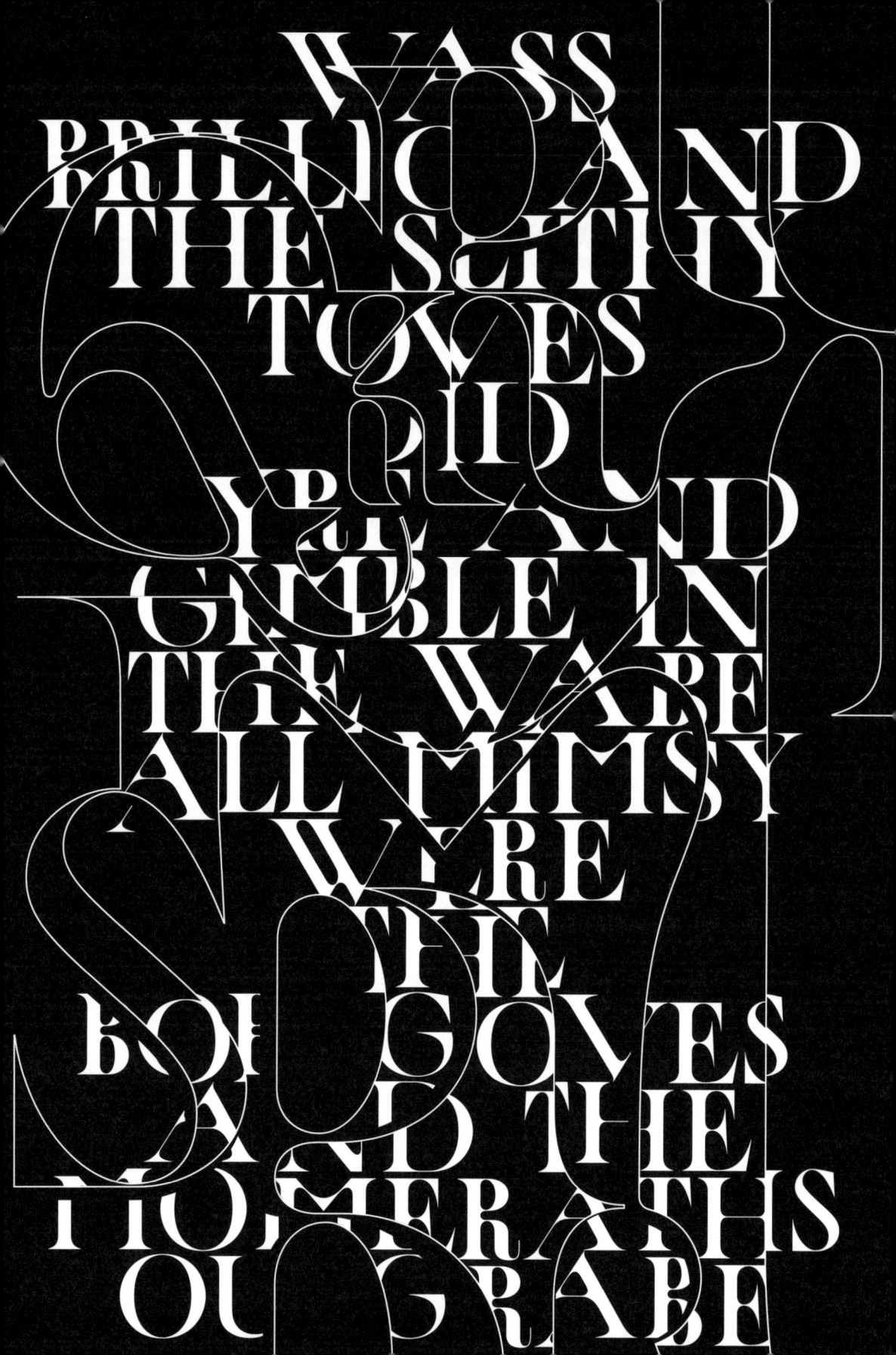

Marquise

Inès Davodeau

INFORMATION
Marquise—La Marquise de Sévigné is one of the most famous women in French literature—is a delicate serif typeface, inspired by the XVII century aesthetic, especially by dress ornaments. Based on a classical Roman structure, the main construction idea was the radical use of teardrop terminals to create the organic decorative look. With that spirit every letter became like little jewellery with delicate details. It is born from a contemporary fantasy look on decorative patterns of the era. Thought as a display typeface, Marquise is meant to be both decorative and functional to bring some preciousness and romanticism to the most beautiful words.

CLASSIFICATION
Display

STYLES
Regular

RELEASE
N/A

CONTACT
inesdavodeau.com
@ines__dv

AND THE QUEEN TAKES THE KING

MBI-Traffic

Fabian Maier-Bode

INFORMATION
MBI-Traffic is a digital revival typeface based on an alphabet from Margaret Calvert which I found in the book "Typography—an encyclopaedic survey of type design and techniques throughout history". Margaret Calvert is a British typographer and graphic designer who is well known for the design of many road signs throughout the United Kingdom. Her alphabet—originally only available in uppercase glyphs—reminds of road marking elements and traffic signs. But there's also a second, different vibe in it. It's somehow cryptic. Like old hieroglyphics. But single elements are hitting the zeitgeist as well. Anyways, these shapes and forms inspired me a lot, so I decided to do a digital revival version of it with slightly changed stylistic details and a complete new lowercase version. The display typeface comes with numbers and a very restricted set of punctuation.

CLASSIFICATION
Display

STYLES
Regular

RELEASE
2022

CONTACT
fabianmaierbode.de
@fabianmaierbode

Megh

Morgane Vantorre

INFORMATION
Driven by the need to move away from screens and return to a tangible manipulation of language, I wanted to design a typeface both digital and wooden (in collaboration with the British engraver Scott Cameron, @typehighdesign) whose rigorously drawn forms could give rise to multiple sets of visual connections both horizontal and vertical. Megh, of which the current state is only a start, is a typeface that finds its balance between metrical rigour and the poetry of form/material sensitivity.

CLASSIFICATION
Lineal

STYLES
Digital
Wood

RELEASE
2021

CONTACT
morganevantorre.com
@gagane_

Meta Mascot

Sangah Shin, Jaejin Ee

INFORMATION
Meta Mascot is a conceptual typeface characterised by an ambiguity between form and letter as a variable font. The project started from our interest in cuteness as the aesthetic of powerlessness, which subverts a relationship between the power and the powerless—and therefore creates ambivalence. Considering that typeface as a way of shaping linguistic identity, we are experimenting anti-linguistic characteristics of cuteness with the concept of morphological uncertainty. General attributes of cute mascots are reflected in this typeface. Every letter from A to Z acts as a single mascot, creating meta mascots when letters are arranged into words. Currently, Meta Mascot is being developed into a variable font by adding different weights. Morphing from the lightest to the heaviest weight, it turns into a formless form and crosses the boundary between shaping and unshaping its letterform—as if jelly, a kind of unrelated eukaryotic organisms, moves constantly in a boundary between liquid and solid.

CLASSIFICATION
Display

STYLES
Mascot Chubby
Mascot Quirky
Mascot Tiny

RELEASE
2019

CONTACT
@sangahakasha
@jae___ee

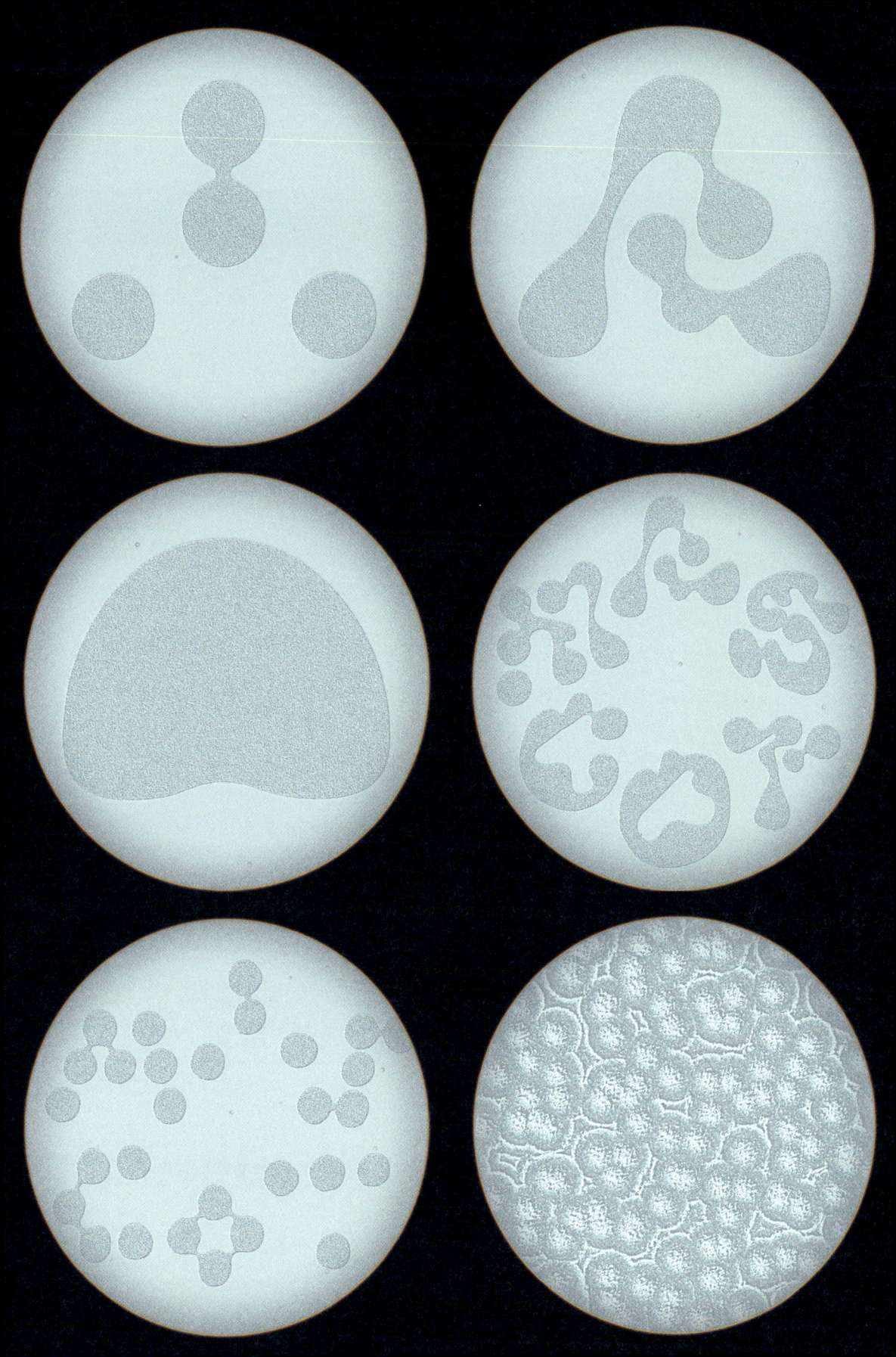

Metamor Bit

Masahiro Naruse

INFORMATION
Metamor Bit is a bitmap style variable font. It is freely available as exported fonts. Additionally, the purchase on Future Fonts comes with an editable Glyphs app file in which you can swap 9 materials, and create your own fonts. (Glyphs 3 itself is not included in the purchase.) This is called Custom Texture Feature, and you can distribute your exported fonts within the purchased license number. Graphically, it's inspired by Postmodernism and Memphis design.

CLASSIFICATION
Display

STYLES
Variable

RELEASE
2021

CONTACT
masahiro-n.com
@rohisamaseruna

METAMORBIT

メタモルビット
かな

A VARIABLE
FONT *FOR*
CJKL #4

MADE IN
NEW YORK

INFORMATION
Mushy is a soft-edged joining script display type that comes in four weights and uses contextual alternates for its joining script. This feature can be turned on and off. The inspiration for Mushy comes from Jugendstil soft display types like Herkules. The idea for the joining script comes from inky textura types (Gutenberg Bible style lettering), where the blackletter in/out strokes bleed into each other and make a line of text look like a garden fence. This drippy sticky look makes Mushy feel organic and tasty. The names for the weights come from the German tradition of associating visual font weight with food products. For example the terms Dreiviertelfett, Halbfett, and so on, are font weights and also descriptions of cheese, butter, margarine etc. Mushy's weight system plays with this idea using the names of dairy products graded in their fat content.

CLASSIFICATION
Display

STYLES
Cream
Yoghurt
Butter
Cheese

RELEASE
2022

CONTACT
lewismcguffie.com
@lewisandhistype

CREAMY
Kabocha
ROASTED
Pumpkins
SAUSAGES
Bubblegum
KOMBUCHA
Caramels
MUSHROOM
Watermelon
GRUYERE
Sprinklings
MILKSHAKE
Marmalade
ORANGES
Honey

Neue Schrift

Daniel Angermann

INFORMATION
Neue Schrift is a modern breaking out headline and display font with aspects of ornamentation based on a monospace character. It is well suited for striking use in large font sizes. Neue Schrift is the attempt to link early processes and points of contact in graffiti painting with my current work. It is based on a spontaneously freely analogue drawn character set which was created and digitalized when I had absolute freedom and wasn't involved in any other project. When you are very close to yourself something can arise that is very different in present.

CLASSIFICATION
Display

STYLES
One Size

RELEASE
2021

CONTACT
daniel-angermann.de

CHARACTER OVERVIEW: 243

TYPEFACE
New Eco

DESIGNER/S
Hyunjun Jang

INFORMATION
New Eco is a typeface that visually interprets natural or organic feelings from a contemporary perspective. It is inspired by images and imagination of the modified nature of the current or in the near future. The name New Eco directly reflects the inspiration and character of the typeface. It shows a straight and strong frame under strict rules, but within that frame it has a contradictory feature by pursuing an organic structure and soft details. These characteristics create graphic and abstract patterns when the letters are written and reinforce their character as a display typeface. Also, in order for this typeface to work effectively as a display typeface, I created an alternative style for almost every glyph, seeking interesting and optimal combinations and variety between letters. Initially, this typeface started as a typeface for a musician, but it was not realised due to personal circumstances, so I completed it independently.

CLASSIFICATION
Display

STYLES
Regular

RELEASE
2020

CONTACT
hyunjunjang.com
@individual_jang

THE
NEW ECO

1

NEW ECOLOGY

A
BC
DEF
GHIJ
KLMNO
PQRSTU
VWXYZ
1234
567
89
0

NEW ECOLOGY NEW ECOLOGY NEW ECOLOGY

YBT

TYPEFACE
New School

DESIGNER/S
Daniel Brokstad

INFORMATION
The general aesthetic is inspired by heavy, condensed and tight sans serif type used on movie posters and music promotional material of the 70s and 80s, which were often sporting some quirky characteristics. The font takes this old school look, modernises it and fuses it with some more contemporary type treatments. Out of this, New School was born. The type features exaggerated yet consistent ink traps, equal to the spacing between letters, so it all comes together nicely as a very tight fit. There's also a good mix of more fluid lines together with the harder and more traditional sans style. Intended for display/headline use.

CLASSIFICATION
Sans Serif

STYLES
Regular

RELEASE
N/A

CONTACT
danielbrokstad.com
@danielbrokstad

Bonnie Tyler

TURN AROUND,

(Every now and then, I fall apart)

11/02

1983

Total Eclipse of the Heart

Written by Jim Steinman

BRIGHT EYES.

Colombia Records

Nikita

Floriane Rousselot

INFORMATION
Preheat in 2020
Lockdown in feverish dreams

Mix with Paris streets letters,
Movies, Graff, Lights
Enter the Void, Fantasia, In the Mood for Love
Until melted
Add a pinch of spicy,
With epic women personification,
Strong and Bold
Hero in all women
Flavour it, with cheeky shapes, incisive

In pinky neon, coat it
Remove from the Heat
Savour it!

I will celebrate it with a daring name
Nikita

CLASSIFICATION
Display

STYLES
Light
Regular

RELEASE
2021

CONTACT
@floriane.rousselot

NÍKÍTA

DELIGHT
SILLY
CHEEKY

TYPEFACE
Offkey

DESIGNER/S
Nicolas Bernklau

INFORMATION

Jazz music means regularities and irregularities. Different rhythm, different textures. Some defined restriction, certain improvisation. Various influences, yet individual voices through personal interpretation. Balance, out of balance, connection, disconnection, centre of gravity, about to fall, on-key, off-key, flats, blue notes, major and minor. The typeface Offkey makes these attributes its centre with an interplay of two styles: Konvex and Konkav.

CLASSIFICATION
Display

STYLES
Konvex
Konkav

RELEASE
2020

CONTACT
nicolasbernklau.de
@nicolasbernklau

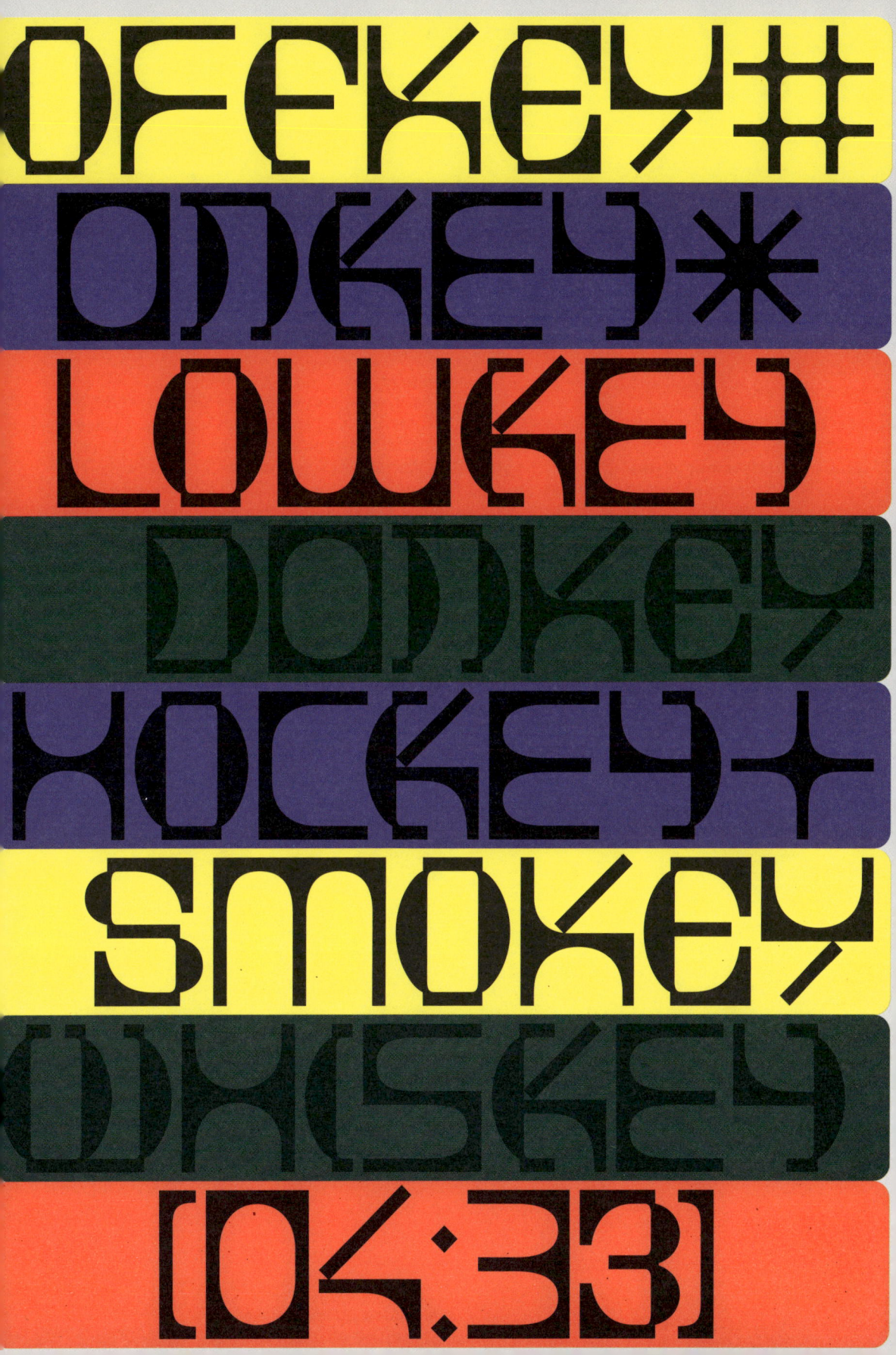

OFEKEY#
ONKEY*
LOWKEY
DONKEY
HOCKEY+
SMOKEY
WHISKEY
[04:33]

TYPEFACE
Quasar

DESIGNER/S
Raoul Gottschling

INFORMATION
Quasar was first used and designed for the interactive journal that is part of Topeka Ogette's "Tupokademie" anti-racism training. If you are a German-speaking person, please read or listen to the audio version of her book "Exit Racism". It'll be an enrichment to your life. The design of Quasar follows a why-the-hell-not-attitude. The punctuation is super bold across all weights, all accents are super light across all weights which results in a play of high and low contrast moments. All characters are the same height. Nothing goes below the baseline or above the cap height. A feature helps achieve crazy tight leading without having to worry about descenders crashing into the line below. Delta is a more circular style, Gamma is more angular, both available with rounded or straight terminals.

CLASSIFICATION
Intergalactic Display

STYLES		
Delta	20	(Rounded)
Gamma	40	(Rounded)
Omni	60	(Rounded)
	80	
	100	
	120	
	140	
	160	
	180	

RELEASE
2022

CONTACT
raoulgottschling.de
@raoulgottschling

CHARACTER OVERVIEW: 248

pästa del
"giörno"
spaghetti
çårbönåra
+ 1 birra
13,70 €

pästa del
"giörno"
spaghetti
çårbönåra
+ 1 birra
13,70 €

TYPEFACE
Rabbit Hole

DESIGNER/S
BOAFFF

INFORMATION
The Rabbit Hole font works perfectly for decorative function. It is mainly dedicated for short titles, for example in magazines. It can also be used for logo creation. Each letter is as twisted as possible but still legible. The lines of the letters do not cross each other. Liquid-like strokes flow seamlessly. The beginning of the letter is also its end, so it reminds me of rabbit ears. Any of the letters can be used individually as a logo-sign. Twisted characters drag you into the hole, the secret world of rabbits. Follow them like Alice in Wonderland.

CLASSIFICATION
Display

STYLES
Regular

RELEASE
2021

CONTACT
hugmun.studio
@boafff

Rapida

Michelangelo Nigra

INFORMATION
Rapida is a serif typeface family distinguished by a mixture of historical conventions and abrupt details that bring energy and sturdiness to the printed sheet. The family started as an investigation of how italic, in relation to the Roman could have been described and shaped across different parameters. The resulting family is a system where the italic itself becomes not just the counterpart of the Roman but a real entity, with its tone of voice, claiming its space. Rapida is characterized by two main sets: the text group, which consists of a Roman plus the correspondingitalic; the display, that presents an extreme visual exploration of the idea of speed, in this case a super fast italic called Rapidissima. Its historical references were Caslon, Fleischmann and Rosart's cuts, which have some parameters I brought into Rapidissima such as high contrast, overall narrow proportions and deep/steep stroke connections.

CLASSIFICATION
Modern Serif

STYLES
Regular
Medium
Bold
Black

RELEASE
2022

CONTACT
@mikenigra

1,026 km, M31 Giant Stream,

B030D $-$ 180 km/s^{-1} [X051,6]

M87 întrebându-l 10,000 s,o

{ "ATM™ [elismişti Text 'i' "}

#on, #€grik, and ¢olon, 9/4

TEMP + At^{-2}/2 the equation!

velōcitās or velōx 2πR/T Eu

340°+(Mike)×(4) Z=[x+i]Y]

Rapidissima Régular Head:

Omegon V-Power 2 Crayford

Tsiolkovsky rocket equation!

Conservation of Momentum

(Princípia Mathematica):

Razor

Carlos Gonçalves

INFORMATION
Razor sharp was developed as the 2021 entry to 36 Days of Type which is a typography challenge that calls for designers from all over the world to showcase their creative exploration and love for typography. It was made from the 5th of April until the 10th of May, each day creating a letter of the alphabet in order. As such the process of making razor sharp started with the character "a" that would set the baseline rules for the letters that would follow. In my case: sharp edges, slightly slanted and high contrast. It evolved with the thought in mind of creating a cohesive set but also being playful with form. It ended up as an exploration/experiment of typography as the challenge had called for.

CLASSIFICATION
Display

STYLES
Regular

RELEASE
2021

CONTACT
@posterkraft

INFORMATION

Relaate is a group of fonts which share certain features, but each of them is much more independent and unique than you would expect from a type family. Each member is an individual: elegant Serif, brutal Slab and quirky tall Grotesque. They treat the family characteristics in different ways, which are more natural for each genre. If you compare such letters as a, e, t, f, r, and many others, you'll see what I mean. This approach allows a wide range of use. The fonts are meant to be used together, independently, or in combinations with others. But Relaate is not a workhorse; actually quite the opposite—a specific type for specific projects. Obviously, its main use is headlines, posters, logotypes and other eye-catching display stuff.

CLASSIFICATION
Old Style Serif
Slab Serif
Grotesque

STYLES
Light
Regular
Medium
Bold
Black
Grotesque
Slab

RELEASE
2019

CONTACT
slobzheninov.com

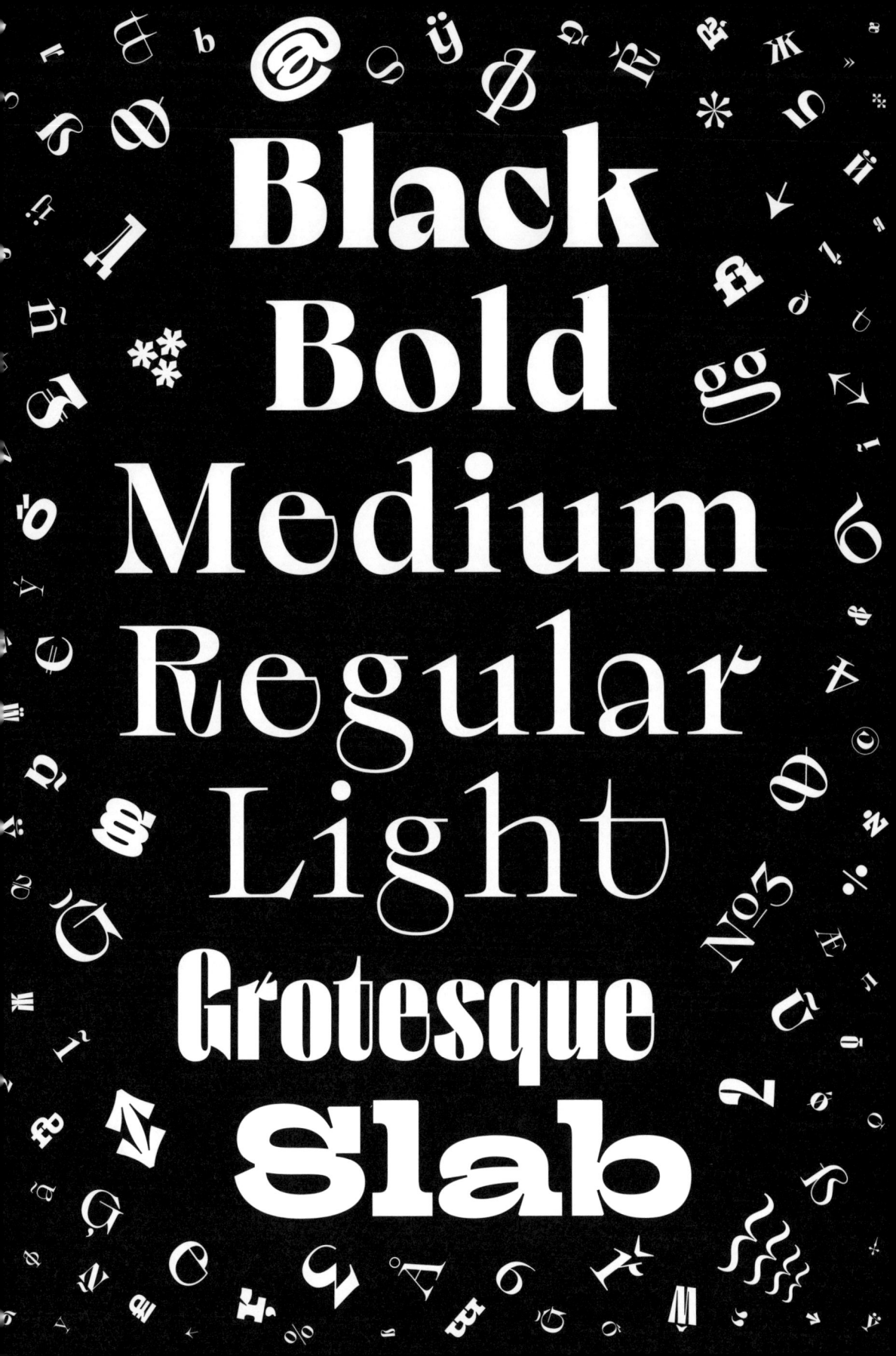

Black
Bold
Medium
Regular
Light
Grotesque
Slab

INFORMATION
Safine is a medium-high contrast, sans-serif display typeface, set for release in 2022. Inspired by the weight of transitional/modern based fonts, early drawings started late 2019 with the aim of creating a straight typeface mixed with some italic characters. The italic "O" and a pure straight "H" were the two main glyphs to develop the whole character set. To balance the wide/expanded feeling of the letters, Safine will feature a second set, more narrowed—to be used separately or combined. Stylistic alternates, with an organic, slightly freestyle treatment will be available for some letters, numbers and punctuation signs. A big set of standard and stylistic ligatures will complete the typeface.

CLASSIFICATION
Display

STYLES
Semibold

RELEASE
2022

CONTACT
@gregory_page_

TYPEFACE
Saint Pierre Nova

DESIGNER/S
Daniel Gremme

INFORMATION
Saint Pierre Nova is the reworked outcome of an academic project at Hochschule Düsseldorf in 2019 and named after a Gothic church in Beauvais. Usually consistency is key when it comes to type design, in this case the opposite rules. Literally shaped out of negative space and playful naivety in just three letter-widths, the typeface contradicts common understandings of typographic construction. Different letter widths break the monoesque appearance from time to time. Historically interrelated glyphs create a rather illustrative image than readable text. Therefore, Saint Pierre Nova is intended to use in large scale. Available in uppercase only, Saint Pierre Nova is still a project in process. Updates with extended glyph-sets will follow.

CLASSIFICATION
Display

STYLES
Nova

RELEASE
2020

CONTACT
danielgremme.com
@danielgremme

Saoirse

Sophia Brinkgerd

INFORMATION
Saoirse was originally initiated and developed in one of my grad school classes at RISD—instructed by Kathleen and Christopher Sleboda—responding to the task of creating a typeface based on a found object. I studied the shapes and formal behaviour of hair. Developing this typeface, I wanted to combine a dynamic lightness and airy feeling, delicate softness as well as a freely flowing motion of the strokes, while still keeping it all within one simple line that would draw each letter. I really liked the challenge of developing contrasts and different levels of complexity within the alphabet, with only using one line stroke, but also maintaining a consistent shape language.

CLASSIFICATION
Display

STYLES
Hairline

RELEASE
2022

CONTACT
sophiabrinkgerd.com
@sophiabrinkgerd

SB Santo

Sascha Bente

INFORMATION
SB Santo is an easy take on stone engravings and inscriptions. I found the original letters on a church wall in Venice and took some photos with my phone. Consequently the font is not an exact revival or an outcome of correct historic research, but rather an illustration of a classically proportioned uppercase-only titling type. Sometimes I like to draw quick stuff like this. The naive 3D effect is to underline Santo's decorative condition. According to the same principle, the name Santo (Holy) can also be read with a wink. All in all, the typeface is a kind of a personal vacation souvenir from Italy.

CLASSIFICATION
Display

STYLES
Outline

RELEASE
2021

CONTACT
saschabente.com
@sascha.bente

CHARACTER OVERVIEW: 256

ASIAGO 5

4 VERDE

FUGASA 7

9 LAGOON

GRANA 12

3 POLENTA

TYPEFACE
Sergio

DESIGNER/S
Jannis Zell

INFORMATION
Sergio was born in a typedesign seminar under the supervision of Philippe Karrer at HfG Karlsruhe. The concept for Sergio is based on graffiti scratchings you can see on windows in the subway for instance. The lines are thin and delicate. Letters overlap each other. Another reference are Italian neon signs, their ligatures and overlapping details. Every letter is drawn by hand trying to use as less strokes as possible (maximum two) while being as fast as needed to create a natural stroke.

CLASSIFICATION
Monoline Script

STYLES
Light

RELEASE
2018

CONTACT
janniszell.com
@janniszell

TYPEFACE
Shakotan

DESIGNER/S
Benoit Brun

INFORMATION
Shakotan refers to a specific and exaggerated style of Japanese tuning. The shape of the letters is inspired by curves from tuned cars, ornaments, and stickers. It suggests motion and fastness. It is a versatile typeface with multiple possible variations for the same letter. Every letter interacts with both the one before and the one after to create a chain composition. My goal was to develop unique combinations that are symbolising movement in visual language.

CLASSIFICATION
Speedy Display

STYLES
Regular

RELEASE
2017

CONTACT
**benoitbrun.com
@benouahh**

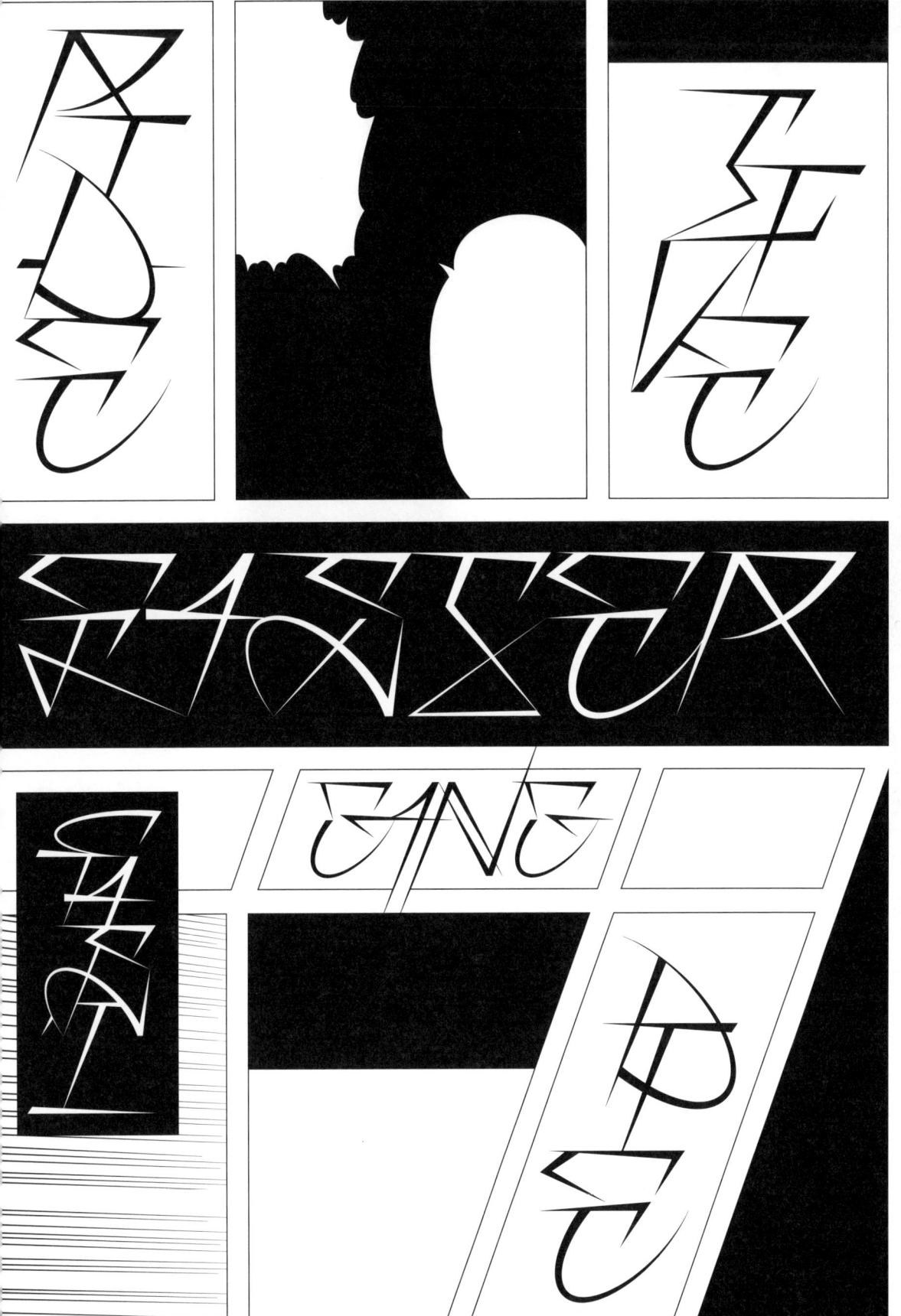

TYPEFACE
Siggy RJ

DESIGNER/S
César Rogers,
Wenrui Zhao

INFORMATION
Siggy RJ was created as a title font for the first issue of the Rietveld Journal, a (mostly) written platform for people who associate with the Gerrit Rietveld Academie. It was initiated by Gersande Schellinx and Irene de Gelder. We tried to achieve democratic design by inviting the editors to share their signatures. In turn, assembling their signatures led us to a typeface which bears the identity of the first issue of Rietveld Journal. Since then, we are collecting signatures for every new issue, so that the typeface updates itself in relation to the people who make the journal.

CLASSIFICATION
Display

STYLES
Regular

RELEASE
2019

CONTACT
@kareslachevresitupeux
@serpenkirt

TYPEFACE
Slime

DESIGNER/S
Wanwai Shum

INFORMATION
Slime is a set of fonts inspired by writing with a pen that almost ran out of ink. Letters are emphasised by the random rhythm of handwriting and overlapping strokes. It is one of the fonts that I have been developing during my personal research on typography, looking for unexpected features which occur in daily behaviour, context and cultural differences.

CLASSIFICATION
Display

STYLES
Bold

RELEASE
2020

CONTACT
@shumww

INFORMATION
During my first year at university, I was asked to design my own typeface. For this I focussed myself on two adjectives: fast and elegant. The serif spikes provide stability and were inspired by the running shoes of athletes. The 1936 Cadillac Shangri-La was the perfect mix of fast and elegant for me, so I decided to use similar shapes for my letters. This is how the Spikes Regular was composed.

CLASSIFICATION
Serif

STYLES
Regular

RELEASE
2021

CONTACT
@alessioborando

Tangerine

Emilie Vizcano

INFORMATION
Tangerine is a serif typeface of approximately 250 glyphs that takes its name from the fruit and its color. At first, It was a lettering sketch. The more the lettering of the word "Tangerine" has progressed, the more the desire has grown on me to make it a full font. It is meant to be elegant, with a Roman inspiration, and a wide range of ligatures. Both soft and sharp, I wanted to draw a typeface that looked like me.

CLASSIFICATION
Serif

STYLES
Courant

RELEASE
2022

CONTACT
emilievizcano.com
@emilievizcano

ABCDE FGHI JKLMN OPQRS TUVW XYZ

abcd efgh ijklmn opq srtuv wxyz

85% WATER
13% CARBOHYDRATES
VITAMIN C (32%)

• Some differ only in disease resistance.
• The term is also currently applied to any reddish orange mandarin

• The peel is thin, with little bitter white mesocarp.
• Tangerine is used fresh or juiced as a spice or zest for baking and drinks.
• The fresh fruit is also used in salads, desserts and main dishes

• Peak tangerine season lasts from autumn to spring.
• Under the former classification system, Citrus tangerina is inside its own separate species.

THE TANGERINE IS A TYPE OF ORANGE.

• All of these traits are shared by mandarins generally.

TAN GE RI NE

TTF OTF WOFF WOFF2 EOT

Tangerines were first grown and cultivated as a distinct crop in the Americas by a Major Atway of Florida. Atway, it is said, tried to import them from Morocco more specifically to their Tangier, which was the origin of the name. Major Atway sold tangerines to N.H. Moragne in 1843, giving the Moragne tangerine the other part of its name.

The Moragne tangerine produced a seedling which became one of the oldest and most popular American varieties, the Dancy tangerine. Tripper-skin tangerine, Kid-glove orange. Genetic analysis has shown the parents of the Dancy is has its own two mandarin orange hybridisms. It is a small easy-to-consumption, a fruition mandarin orange and a sanguri mandarin orange.

The Dancy is no longer widely commercially grown, it is too delicate to handle and ship well. It is too susceptible to Alternaria fungus, and it bears more heavily in alternate years. Dancy is still grown for personal consumption, and many hybrids of the Dancy are grown commercially.

Tondo

Nicolò Oriani

INFORMATION
In a playful sense, Tondo means circle in Italian slang. The word is also related to the process of building a modular character through the use of three simple geometric shapes: the circle, the rounded rectangle and a thin line. The latter two shapes make up the design of the letter by digging inside the basic shape of the circle. The font is designed as a single family and is the result of a typographical research that is based on pushing extreme letters to the limits of its readability.

CLASSIFICATION
Modular Display

STYLES
Regular

RELEASE
2020

CONTACT
@nicolooriani

Toothpick

Kasper Pyndt

INFORMATION

The inspiration for Toothpick comes from a very material notion of making structures by adhering pieces of wood together. I was intrigued by the appearance of continuing strokes past their connecting points. This was only really visually viable in a very thin weight—applying the trait in a bolder weight caused a much less defined expression and extremely inky intersections. For that reason, Toothpick is an unapologetically one-weight, geometric display font. One of its primary qualities has to be the very disparate expressions it can achieve depending on size. In large headlines it's jagged, unpolished and in-your-face. In smaller sizes (minimum 15 pt is recommended) its ink traps and rough intricacies create a very satisfying texture that almost causes a paragraph to optically sparkle. A colleague called it "a typeface for scouts" which somehow nails it. However, the name Toothpick felt pretty obvious, too.

CLASSIFICATION
Modular

STYLES
Thin

RELEASE
2021

CONTACT
approxtype.com
@approx.type

CHARACTER OVERVIEW: 264

STICKS AND STONES MAY BREAK MY BONES

ALL ORGANIC MATERIALS

THRIFTY SCOUTS

RITUALS? BONFIRE WITCH

1-01

TOOTHPICK

BLAIR

ALL ORGANIC MATERIALS SUPPOSEDLY A FONT FOR THRIFTY OR TOOTHPICK

INFORMATION
While working on a bespoke typeface for Campari, I stumbled upon a magazine called "Le vie d'Italia" which was published monthly by Touring Club Italiano between 1917 and 1968. From 1924 to 1933 it was expanded and published under the name "Le Vie d'Italia e dell'America Latina". Toy emerged from its vivid title lettering. An uncommon C_A ligature and the alternate letter combination L_A provided the starting point for a tight headline typeface pushing the concept of ligatures to its limit. With connected script typefaces in mind, letters were designed for ultra tight letter treatment. Even larger amounts of negative letter spacing do not break the rhythm but letters mesh with each other nicely. Where necessary, OpenType kicks in with more than one hundred ligatures, contextual alternates and space saving superior/inferior letter combinations. The design of letters with descenders and very compact accents provide possibilities for extra tight line spacing.

CLASSIFICATION
Experimental Display

STYLES
Regular

RELEASE
2020

CONTACT
outofthedark.xyz
@outofthedark.xyz

COBRAS

✳ J DILLA

THIRTEEN

CRIP-WALK

ESTABLISHED

NEIGHBORHOOD

Chicago, Illinois U.S. 74

#OUTOFTHEDARKTYPEFACES

INFORMATION
I started working on Transit in late 2017 in my spare time beside a full-time job at a graphic design studio. As spare time was quite rare those days, the process took me quite a long time and there were breaks of several months in between. Despite that, development has never stopped over the years and the typeface has absorbed different influences. A decisive point in the design process was the look of the lower case letter "t", which probably is a bit unusual. I found it very interesting and tried to adapt the idea to more letters and started experimenting with the shapes which resulted in interesting combinations, ligatures and alternates. In consequence, the typeface got a new direction and a more and more organic feeling. Transit is still in progress and an update with more styles is planned for the near future.

CLASSIFICATION
Grotesk

STYLES
Regular

RELEASE
2021

CONTACT
robert-gutmann.com
@robert_gutmann

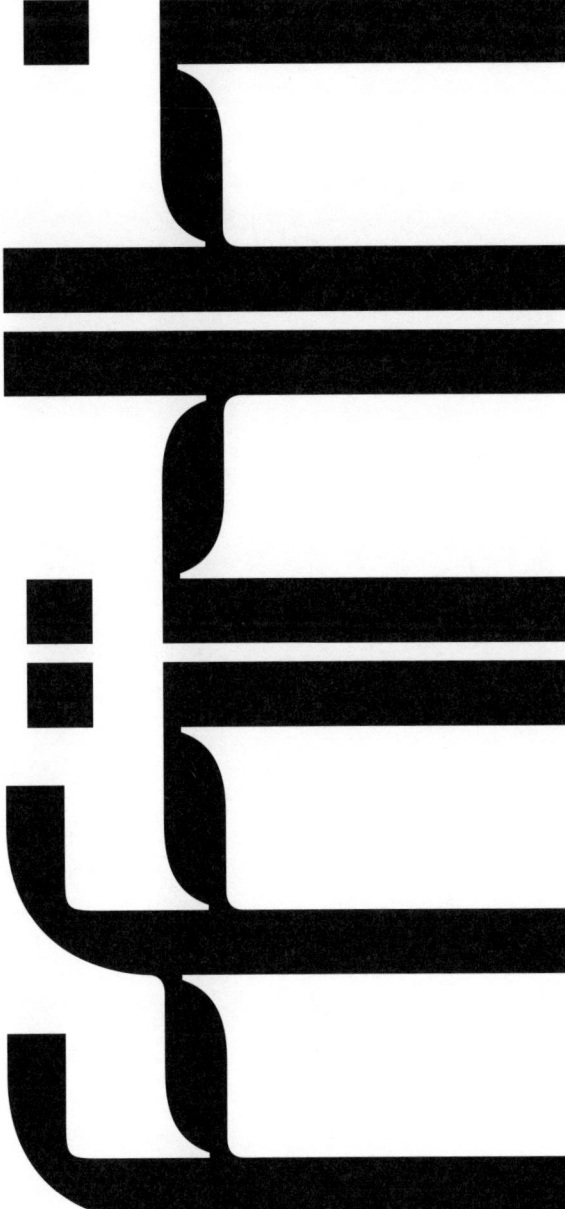

transit^{TTC}

Made in ○ Europe

New Æsthetic

UBU Habak

Adam Asztalos

INFORMATION
UBU Habak is a display typeface based on a cal-
ligraphy I did at the end of 2017. The calligraphy itself was just a word: absztinencia (abstinence).
Few months after drawing it, I jumped into digitising and expanding it to a whole alphabet. First,
I did only lowercase letters. Almost a year later, I added capitals and numbers to it. Maybe a year
ago, I added three weights, too (skinny, almost there, thick). The special characteristics of the
font are the thick and curvy lines. The thickness stays the same everywhere except at sharp turns
and junctions where it is a bit thinner. Habak is ideal for screwing up your projects, making your
momma cry or even ruining your whole design career.

CLASSIFICATION
Variable Monospace Display

STYLES
Neocalligraphy

RELEASE
N/A

CONTACT
uglybutuseless.com
@uglybutuseless

VELOCE

Robin Pitchon

INFORMATION
VELOCE is a futuristic, Swiss style and 90's sci-fi inspired display typeface that comes in one regular weight. It is built from geometric parts and is better used at big sizes. The typeface covers letters, numbers and symbols, and is perfect for creating a short logotype or monogram. Moreover, VELOCE is built according to a rather short template, so it can be used both as upper and lower case. The 24 ligatures allow you to play with alternate versions of your letters and create unique letters combinations.

CLASSIFICATION
Display

STYLES
Regular

RELEASE
2021

CONTACT
olohgram.com
@olohgram

INFORMATION
VZWO VOL is designed and realised by Viktor Zumegen. It is a variable font family that consists of 27 styles in its base, 9 volumes, each available in upright, slanted and backslanted. With two sliders it is possible to set the volume between 010 and 102 units and the slant between -12 and 12 degrees. The duplex design of the volumes thus gives the users a wide range of design options and maximum control—from hair-thin screen dots to solid, punched letters; from backslanted over Roman to slanted.

CLASSIFICATION
Variable Display

STYLES
010
013
018
024
032
043
057
076
102

Slanted
Backslanted
Variable

RELEASE
2022

CONTACT
viktorzumegen.de
@viktorzumegen

VIDIO VOL!

BY VIDIO|VIKTOR ZIMEGIN ++++

[UPRIGHT]

TYPEFACE
Wagnis

DESIGNER/S
Mike Dziambor

INFORMATION
Wagnis is inspired by the imperfections of the daring experiment the typeface is itself. Every glyph was made first try using the path tool. Without any sort of grid or rules, Wagnis aims to be a modern, provocative, yet fascinating type design. With spiky edges and irregular sizing, it is supposed to look like a mistake, yet the aesthetic is so unique and interesting that you want to take a closer look at every single glyph.

CLASSIFICATION
Display

STYLES
Irregular

RELEASE
2021

CONTACT
mikedziambor.com
@mikedziambor

Westenwind

Olga Umpeleva

INFORMATION
Westenwind (Dutch for west wind) was a part of my graduation project at the Type and Media master course at KABK. It is inspired by the wind in the Netherlands which is able to blow in all different directions at the same time. And Westenwind started with a simple observation. There are not enough serifs in our typefaces. Why should serifs only be present in certain places? Why is it not possible to add them elsewhere? Later I thought that if bolder styles usually have bigger ink traps and different kinds of compensations, then maybe the black wide style also needs more ink traps? Both styles have glyphs with left and right serifs, so it is possible to adjust the lengths of serifs on the left or right side of a letter separately. Westenwind's aim is to question type design classification and rules—and inspire designers to break them.

CLASSIFICATION
Display

STYLES
Black Wide
Light Narrow

RELEASE
2021

CONTACT
olgaumpeleva.com
@olga.umpeleva

0041	0042	0043	0044	0045	0046	0047	0048	0049	004A
004B	004C	004D	004E	004F	0050	0051	0052	0053	0054
0055	0056	0057	0058	0059	005A				
0061	0062	0063	0064	0065	0066	0067	0068	0069	006A
006B	006C	006D	006E	006F	0070	0071	0072	0073	0074
0075	0076	0077	0078	0079	007A				
0031	0032	0033	0034	0035	0036	0037	0038	0039	0030
0028	0021	0023	0024	0025	0026	002A	003F	0040	0029

0041	0042	0043	0044	0045	0046	0047	0048	0049	004A
004B	004C	004D	004E	004F	0050	0051	0052	0053	0054
0055	0056	0057	0058	0059	005A				
0061	0062	0063	0064	0065	0066	0067	0068	0069	006A
006B	006C	006D	006E	006F	0070	0071	0072	0073	0074
0075	0076	0077	0078	0079	007A				
0031	0032	0033	0034	0035	0036	0037	0038	0039	0030
0028	0021	0023	0024	0025	0026	002A	003F	0040	0029

DATA SHEET: 10

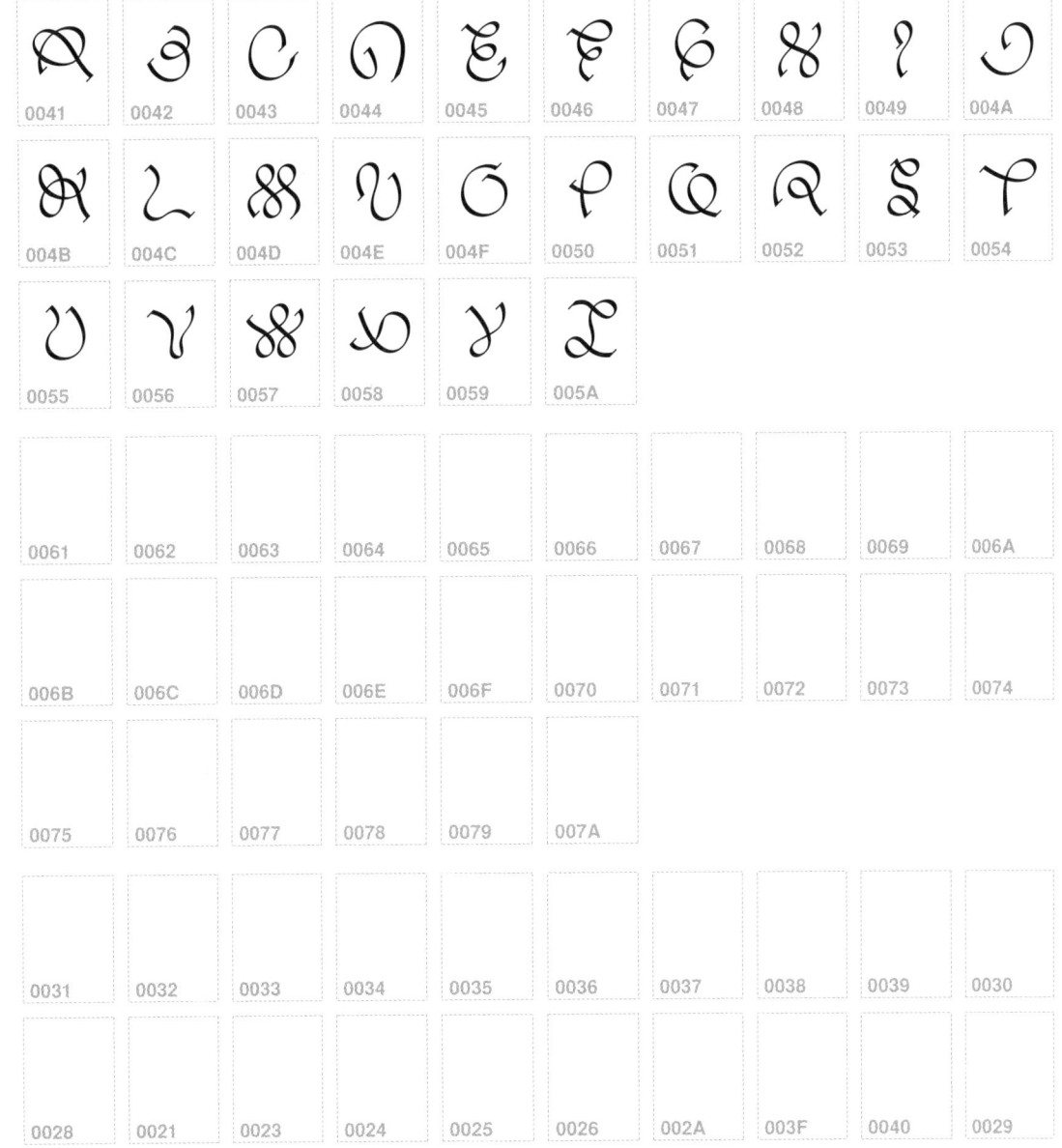

0041	0042	0043	0044	0045	0046	0047	0048	0049	004A
004B	004C	004D	004E	004F	0050	0051	0052	0053	0054
0055	0056	0057	0058	0059	005A				
0061	0062	0063	0064	0065	0066	0067	0068	0069	006A
006B	006C	006D	006E	006F	0070	0071	0072	0073	0074
0075	0076	0077	0078	0079	007A				
0031	0032	0033	0034	0035	0036	0037	0038	0039	0030
0028	0021	0023	0024	0025	0026	002A	003F	0040	0029

DATA SHEET: 12

A 0041	B 0042	C 0043	D 0044	E 0045	F 0046	G 0047	H 0048	I 0049	J 004A
K 004B	L 004C	M 004D	N 004E	O 004F	P 0050	Q 0051	R 0052	S 0053	T 0054
U 0055	V 0056	W 0057	X 0058	Y 0059	Z 005A				
a 0061	b 0062	c 0063	d 0064	e 0065	f 0066	g 0067	h 0068	i 0069	j 006A
k 006B	l 006C	m 006D	n 006E	o 006F	p 0070	q 0071	r 0072	s 0073	t 0074
u 0075	v 0076	w 0077	x 0078	y 0079	z 007A				
1 0031	2 0032	3 0033	4 0034	5 0035	6 0036	7 0037	8 0038	9 0039	0 0030
(0028	! 0021	# 0023	§ 0024	% 0025	& 0026	* 002A	? 003F	@ 0040	) 0029

0041	0042	0043	0044	0045	0046	0047	0048	0049	004A
004B	004C	004D	004E	004F	0050	0051	0052	0053	0054
0055	0056	0057	0058	0059	005A				
0061	0062	0063	0064	0065	0066	0067	0068	0069	006A
006B	006C	006D	006E	006F	0070	0071	0072	0073	0074
0075	0076	0077	0078	0079	007A				
0031	0032	0033	0034	0035	0036	0037	0038	0039	0030
0028	0021	0023	0024	0025	0026	002A	003F	0040	0029

A 0041	B 0042	C 0043	D 0044	E 0045	F 0046	G 0047	H 0048	I 0049	J 004A
K 004B	L 004C	M 004D	N 004E	O 004F	P 0050	Q 0051	R 0052	S 0053	T 0054
U 0055	V 0056	W 0057	X 0058	Y 0059	Z 005A				
a 0061	b 0062	c 0063	d 0064	e 0065	f 0066	g 0067	h 0068	i 0069	j 006A
k 006B	l 006C	m 006D	n 006E	o 006F	p 0070	q 0071	r 0072	s 0073	t 0074
u 0075	v 0076	w 0077	x 0078	y 0079	z 007A				
1 0031	2 0032	3 0033	4 0034	5 0035	6 0036	7 0037	8 0038	9 0039	0 0030
(0028	! 0021	# 0023	§ 0024	0025	& 0026	✳ 002A	? 003F	@ 0040	) 0029

A	B	C	D	E	F	G	H	I	J
0041	0042	0043	0044	0045	0046	0047	0048	0049	004A
K	L	M	N	O	P	Q	R	S	T
004B	004C	004D	004E	004F	0050	0051	0052	0053	0054
U	V	W	X	Y	Z				
0055	0056	0057	0058	0059	005A				
a	b	c	d	e	f	g	h	i	j
0061	0062	0063	0064	0065	0066	0067	0068	0069	006A
k	l	m	n	o	p	q	r	s	t
006B	006C	006D	006E	006F	0070	0071	0072	0073	0074
u	v	w	x	y	z				
0075	0076	0077	0078	0079	007A				
1	2	3	4	5	6	7	8	9	0
0031	0032	0033	0034	0035	0036	0037	0038	0039	0030
(	!	#				*	?		)
0028	0021	0023	0024	0025	0026	002A	003F	0040	0029

DATA SHEET: 20

A	B	C	D	E	F	G	H	I	J
0041	0042	0043	0044	0045	0046	0047	0048	0049	004A

K	L	M	N	O	P	Q	R	S	T
004B	004C	004D	004E	004F	0050	0051	0052	0053	0054

U	V	W	X	Y	Z
0055	0056	0057	0058	0059	005A

a	b	c	d	e	f	g	h	i	j
0061	0062	0063	0064	0065	0066	0067	0068	0069	006A

k	l	m	n	o	p	q	r	s	t
006B	006C	006D	006E	006F	0070	0071	0072	0073	0074

u	v	w	x	y	z
0075	0076	0077	0078	0079	007A

1	2	3	4	5	6	7	8	9	0
0031	0032	0033	0034	0035	0036	0037	0038	0039	0030

(	!	#	§	%	&	*	?	@	)
0028	0021	0023	0024	0025	0026	002A	003F	0040	0029

A	B	C	D	E	F	G	H	I	J
0041	0042	0043	0044	0045	0046	0047	0048	0049	004A
K	L	M	N	O	P	Q	R	S	T
004B	004C	004D	004E	004F	0050	0051	0052	0053	0054
U	V	W	X	Y	Z				
0055	0056	0057	0058	0059	005A				
0061	0062	0063	0064	0065	0066	0067	0068	0069	006A
006B	006C	006D	006E	006F	0070	0071	0072	0073	0074
0075	0076	0077	0078	0079	007A				
1	2	3	4	5	6	7	8	9	0
0031	0032	0033	0034	0035	0036	0037	0038	0039	0030
(	!	#					?		)
0028	0021	0023	0024	0025	0026	002A	003F	0040	0029

DATA SHEET: 24

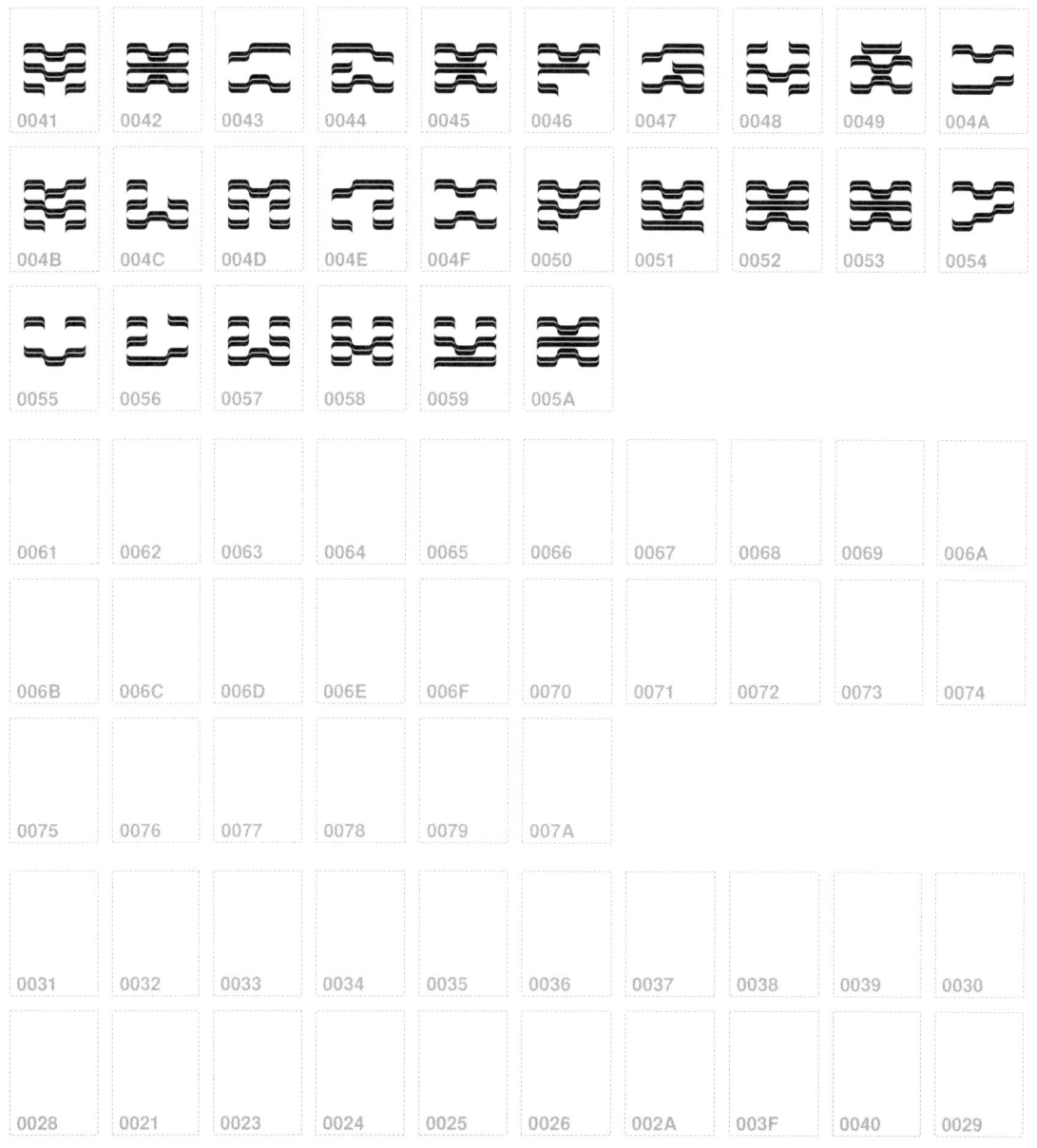

A	B	C	D	E	F	G	H	I	J
0041	0042	0043	0044	0045	0046	0047	0048	0049	004A
K	L	M	N	O	P	Q	R	S	T
004B	004C	004D	004E	004F	0050	0051	0052	0053	0054
U	V	W	X	Y	Z				
0055	0056	0057	0058	0059	005A				

a	b	c	d	e	f	g	h	i	j
0061	0062	0063	0064	0065	0066	0067	0068	0069	006A
k	l	m	n	o	p	q	r	s	t
006B	006C	006D	006E	006F	0070	0071	0072	0073	0074
u	v	w	x	y	z				
0075	0076	0077	0078	0079	007A				

1	2	3	4	5	6	7	8	9	0
0031	0032	0033	0034	0035	0036	0037	0038	0039	0030

(	!	#			&	*	?	@	)
0028	0021	0023	0024	0025	0026	002A	003F	0040	0029

A	B	C	D	E	F	G	H	I	J
0041	0042	0043	0044	0045	0046	0047	0048	0049	004A
K	L	M	N	O	P	Q	R	S	T
004B	004C	004D	004E	004F	0050	0051	0052	0053	0054
U	V	W	X	Y	Z				
0055	0056	0057	0058	0059	005A				
a	b	c	d	e	f	g	h	i	j
0061	0062	0063	0064	0065	0066	0067	0068	0069	006A
k	l	m	n	o	p	q	r	s	t
006B	006C	006D	006E	006F	0070	0071	0072	0073	0074
u	v	w	x	y	z				
0075	0076	0077	0078	0079	007A				
1	2	3	4	5	6	7	8	9	0
0031	0032	0033	0034	0035	0036	0037	0038	0039	0030
[	l	#	§	%	&	*	?	@	]
0028	0021	0023	0024	0025	0026	002A	003F	0040	0029

TYPEFACE
Chalet Girl

DESIGNER/S
Harry Bennett,
Jack Niblett

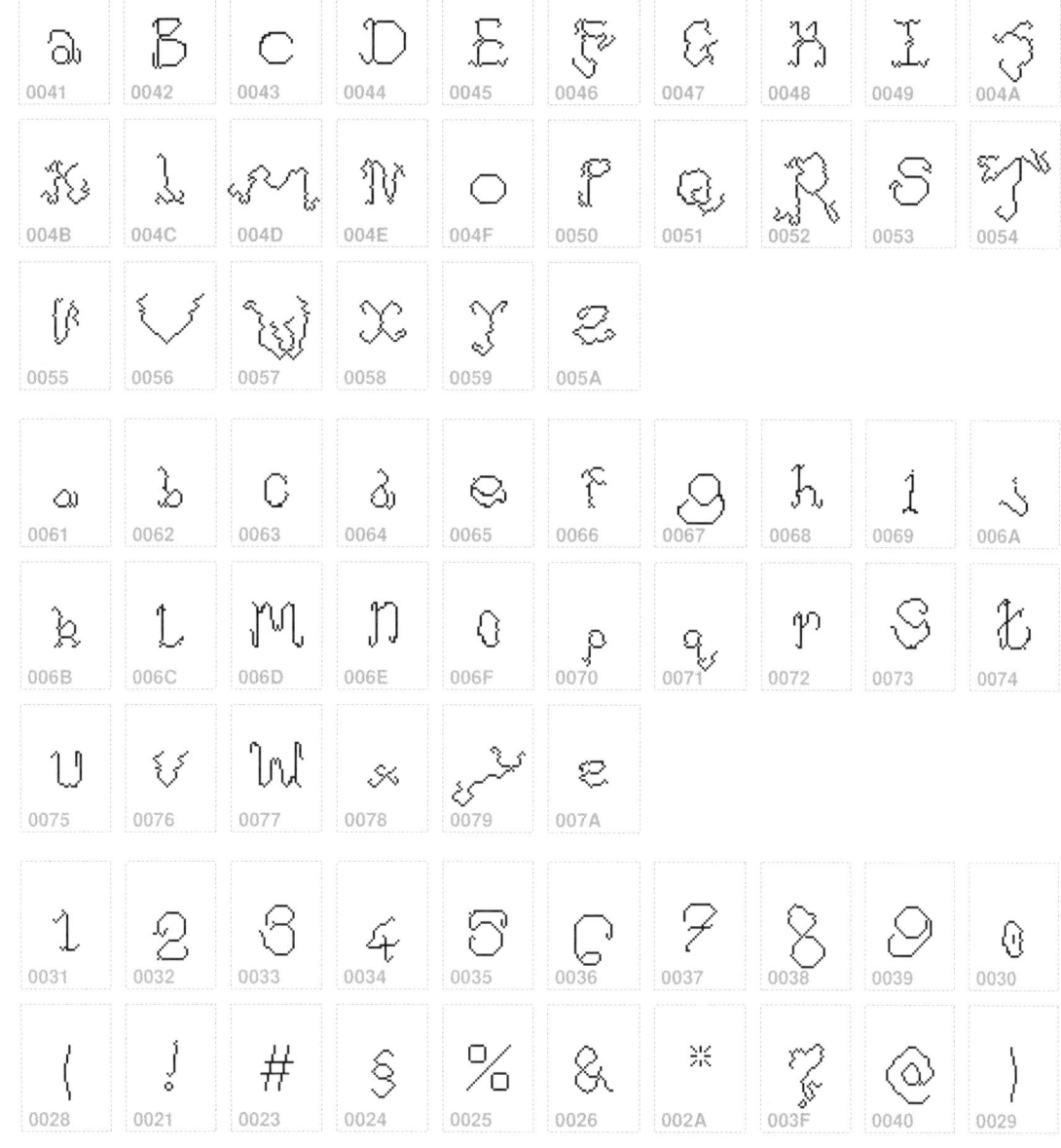

0041	0042	0043	0044	0045	0046	0047	0048	0049	004A
004B	004C	004D	004E	004F	0050	0051	0052	0053	0054
0055	0056	0057	0058	0059	005A				
0061	0062	0063	0064	0065	0066	0067	0068	0069	006A
006B	006C	006D	006E	006F	0070	0071	0072	0073	0074
0075	0076	0077	0078	0079	007A				
0031	0032	0033	0034	0035	0036	0037	0038	0039	0030
0028	0021	0023	0024	0025	0026	002A	003F	0040	0029

0041	0042	0043	0044	0045	0046	0047	0048	0049	004A
004B	004C	004D	004E	004F	0050	0051	0052	0053	0054
0055	0056	0057	0058	0059	005A				
0061	0062	0063	0064	0065	0066	0067	0068	0069	006A
006B	006C	006D	006E	006F	0070	0071	0072	0073	0074
0075	0076	0077	0078	0079	007A				
0031	0032	0033	0034	0035	0036	0037	0038	0039	0030
0028	0021	0023	0024	0025	0026	002A	003F	0040	0029

TYPEFACE
CirrusCumulus

DESIGNER/S
Clara Sambot

0041	0042	0043	0044	0045	0046	0047	0048	0049	004A
004B	004C	004D	004E	004F	0050	0051	0052	0053	0054
0055	0056	0057	0058	0059	005A				
0061	0062	0063	0064	0065	0066	0067	0068	0069	006A
006B	006C	006D	006E	006F	0070	0071	0072	0073	0074
0075	0076	0077	0078	0079	007A				
0031	0032	0033	0034	0035	0036	0037	0038	0039	0030
0028	0021	0023	0024	0025	0026	002A	003F	0040	0029

DATA SHEET: 36

0041	0042	0043	0044	0045	0046	0047	0048	0049	004A
004B	004C	004D	004E	004F	0050	0051	0052	0053	0054
0055	0056	0057	0058	0059	005A				
0061	0062	0063	0064	0065	0066	0067	0068	0069	006A
006B	006C	006D	006E	006F	0070	0071	0072	0073	0074
0075	0076	0077	0078	0079	007A				
0031	0032	0033	0034	0035	0036	0037	0038	0039	0030
0028	0021	0023	0024	0025	0026	002A	003F	0040	0029

A	B	C	D	E	F	G	H	I	J
0041	0042	0043	0044	0045	0046	0047	0048	0049	004A

K	L	M	N	O	P	Q	R	S	T
004B	004C	004D	004E	004F	0050	0051	0052	0053	0054

U	V	W	X	Y	Z
0055	0056	0057	0058	0059	005A

a	b	c	d	e	f	g	h	i	j
0061	0062	0063	0064	0065	0066	0067	0068	0069	006A

k	l	m	n	o	p	q	r	s	t
006B	006C	006D	006E	006F	0070	0071	0072	0073	0074

u	v	w	x	y	z
0075	0076	0077	0078	0079	007A

1	2	3	4	5	6	7	8	9	0
0031	0032	0033	0034	0035	0036	0037	0038	0039	0030

(	!	#			&	✲	?	@	)
0028	0021	0023	0024	0025	0026	002A	003F	0040	0029

TYPEFACE
Cosmogonia

DESIGNER/S
Leonhard Laupichler

0041	0042	0043	0044	0045	0046	0047	0048	0049	004A
004B	004C	004D	004E	004F	0050	0051	0052	0053	0054
0055	0056	0057	0058	0059	005A				
0061	0062	0063	0064	0065	0066	0067	0068	0069	006A
006B	006C	006D	006E	006F	0070	0071	0072	0073	0074
0075	0076	0077	0078	0079	007A				
0031	0032	0033	0034	0035	0036	0037	0038	0039	0030
0028	0021	0023	0024	0025	0026	002A	003F	0040	0029

DATA SHEET: 42

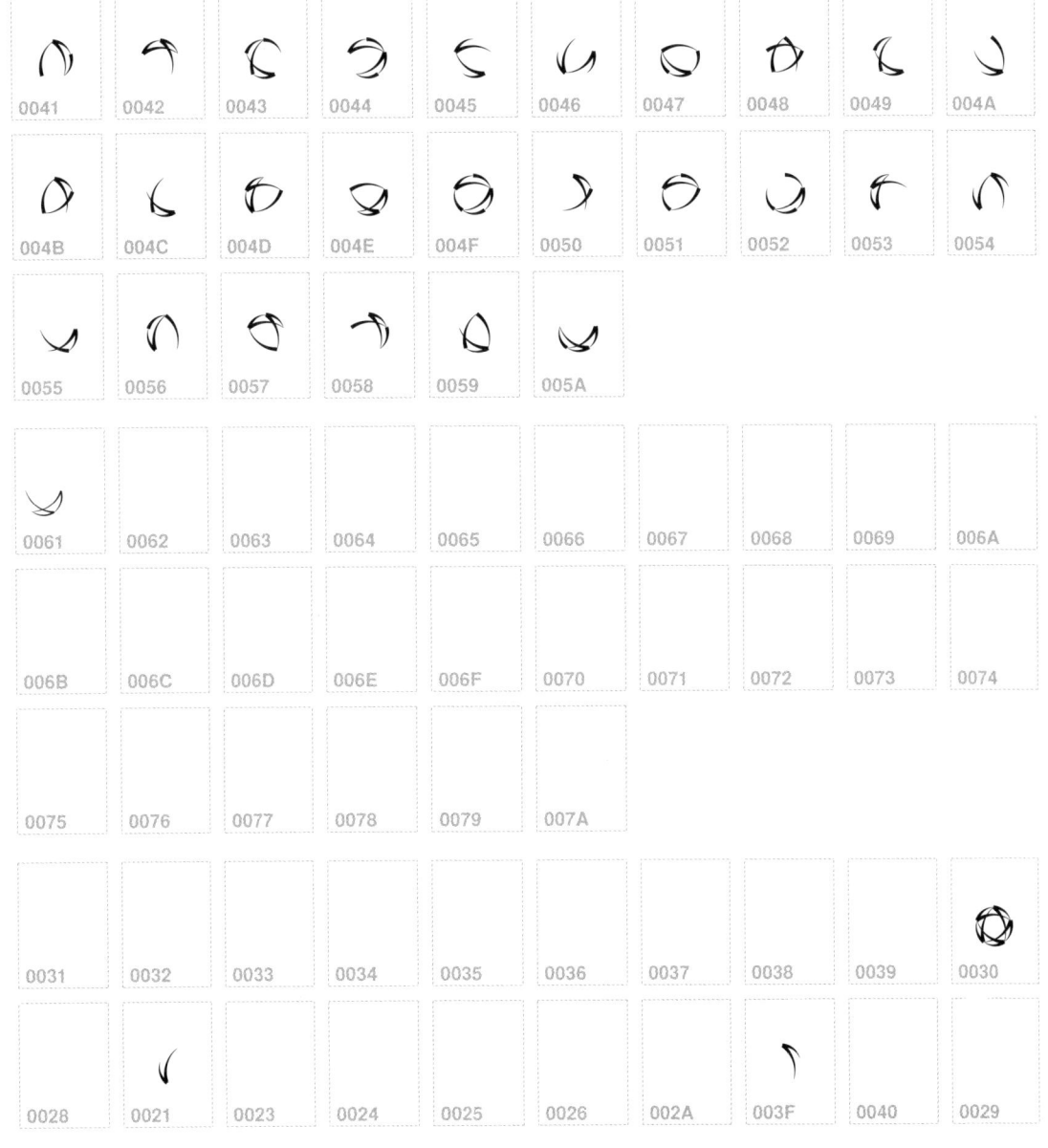

0041	0042	0043	0044	0045	0046	0047	0048	0049	004A
004B	004C	004D	004E	004F	0050	0051	0052	0053	0054
0055	0056	0057	0058	0059	005A				
0061	0062	0063	0064	0065	0066	0067	0068	0069	006A
006B	006C	006D	006E	006F	0070	0071	0072	0073	0074
0075	0076	0077	0078	0079	007A				
0031	0032	0033	0034	0035	0036	0037	0038	0039	0030
0028	0021	0023	0024	0025	0026	002A	003F	0040	0029

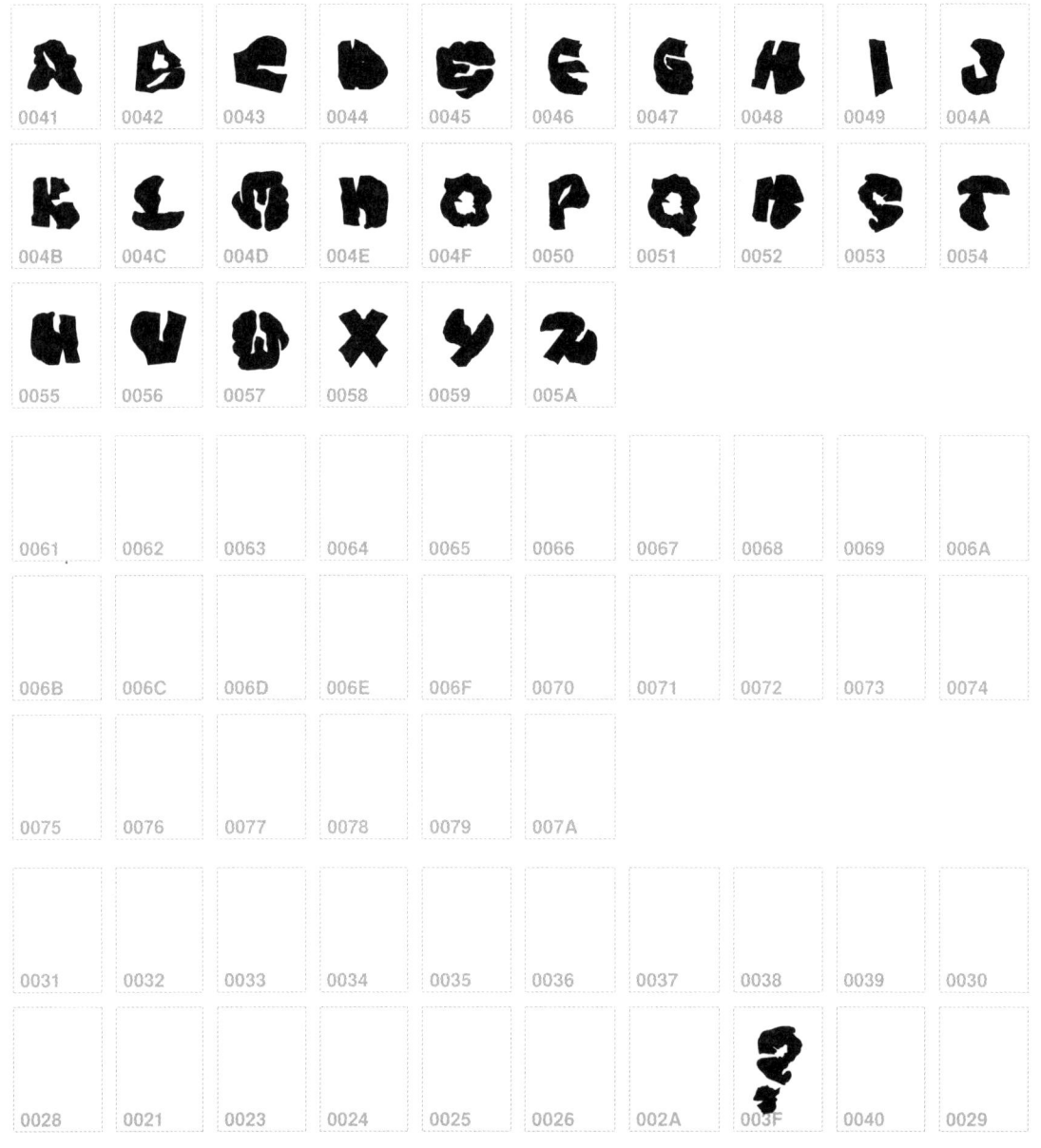

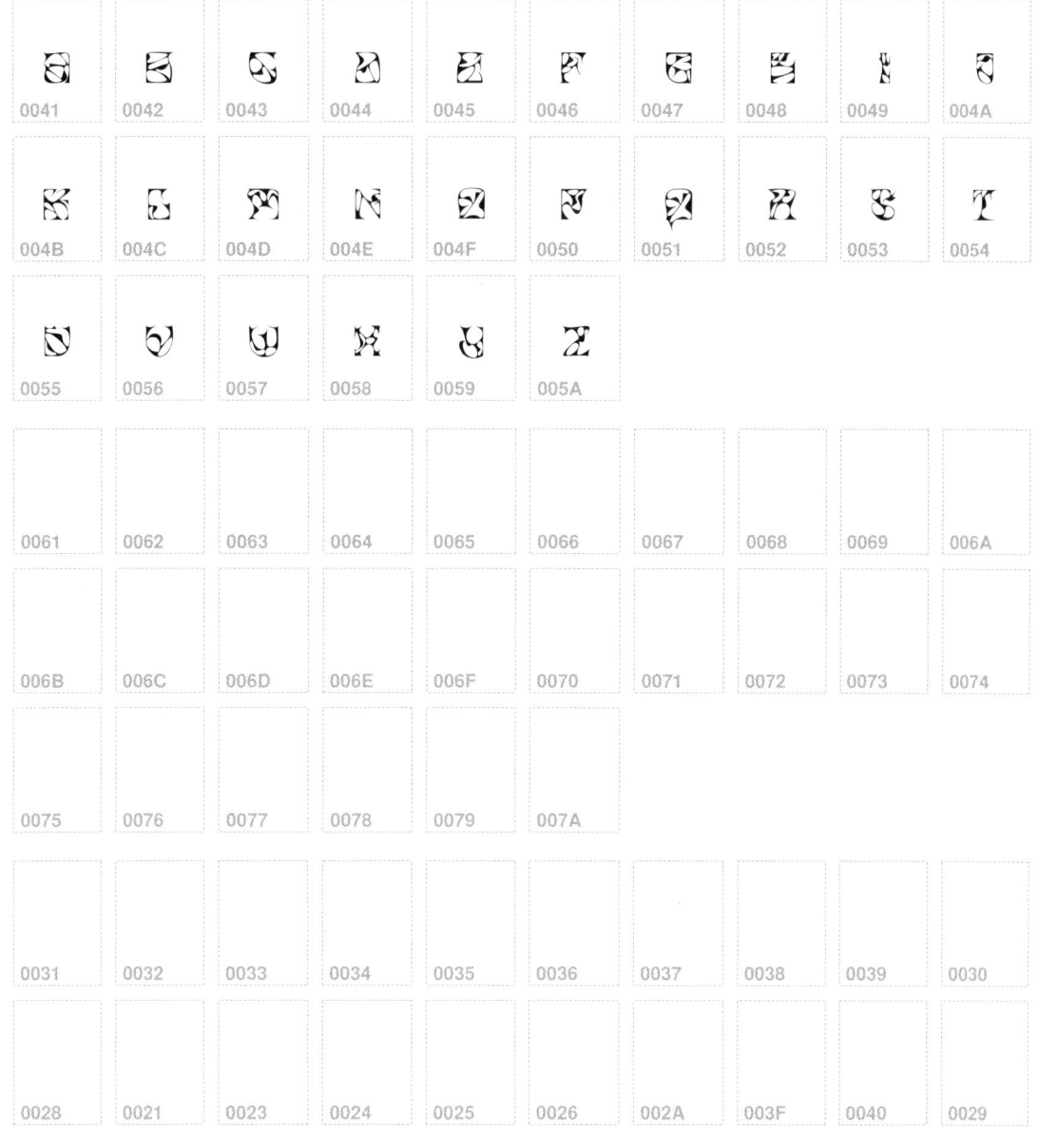

0041	0042	0043	0044	0045	0046	0047	0048	0049	004A
004B	004C	004D	004E	004F	0050	0051	0052	0053	0054
0055	0056	0057	0058	0059	005A				
0061	0062	0063	0064	0065	0066	0067	0068	0069	006A
006B	006C	006D	006E	006F	0070	0071	0072	0073	0074
0075	0076	0077	0078	0079	007A				
0031	0032	0033	0034	0035	0036	0037	0038	0039	0030
0028	0021	0023	0024	0025	0026	002A	003F	0040	0029

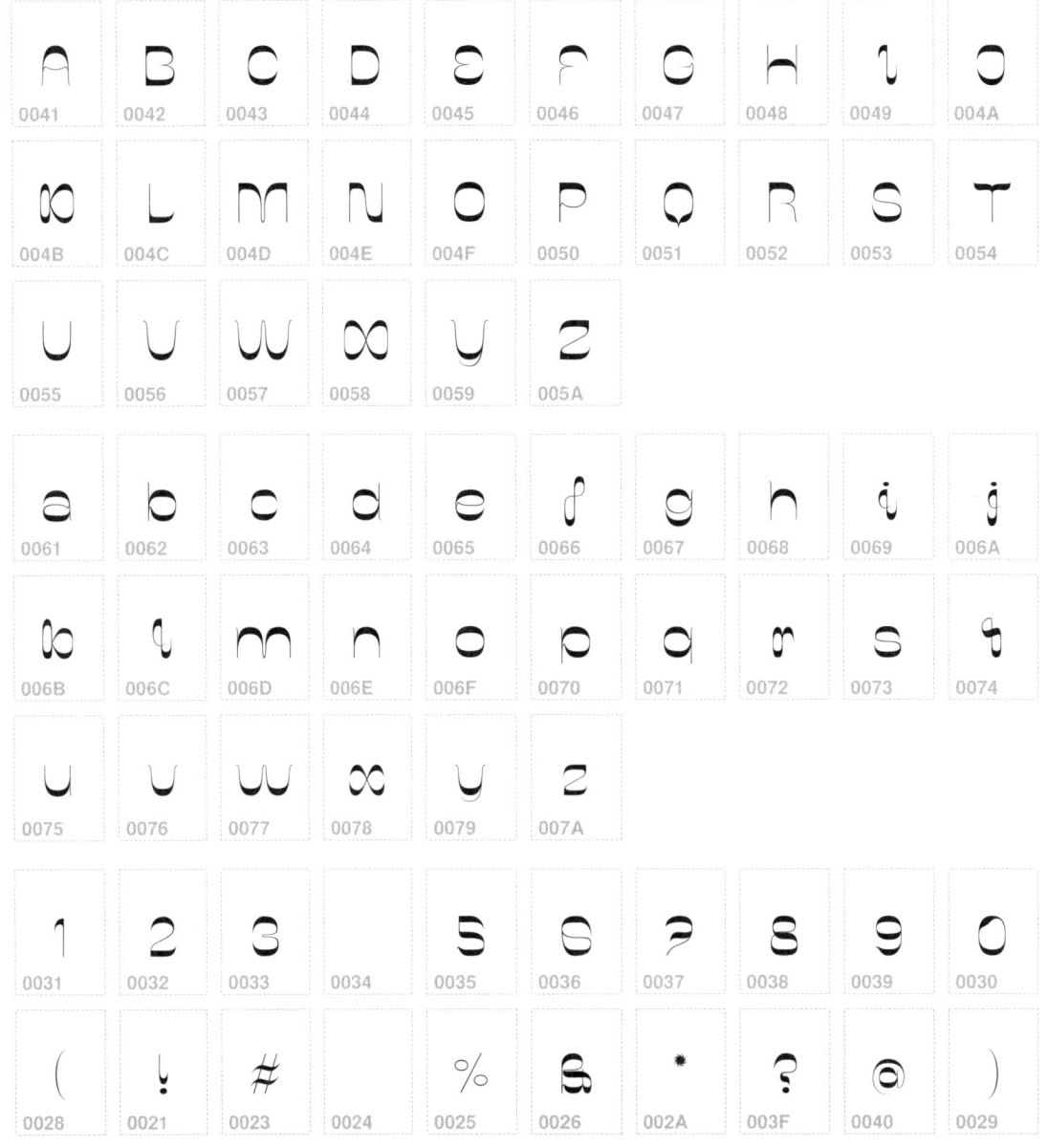

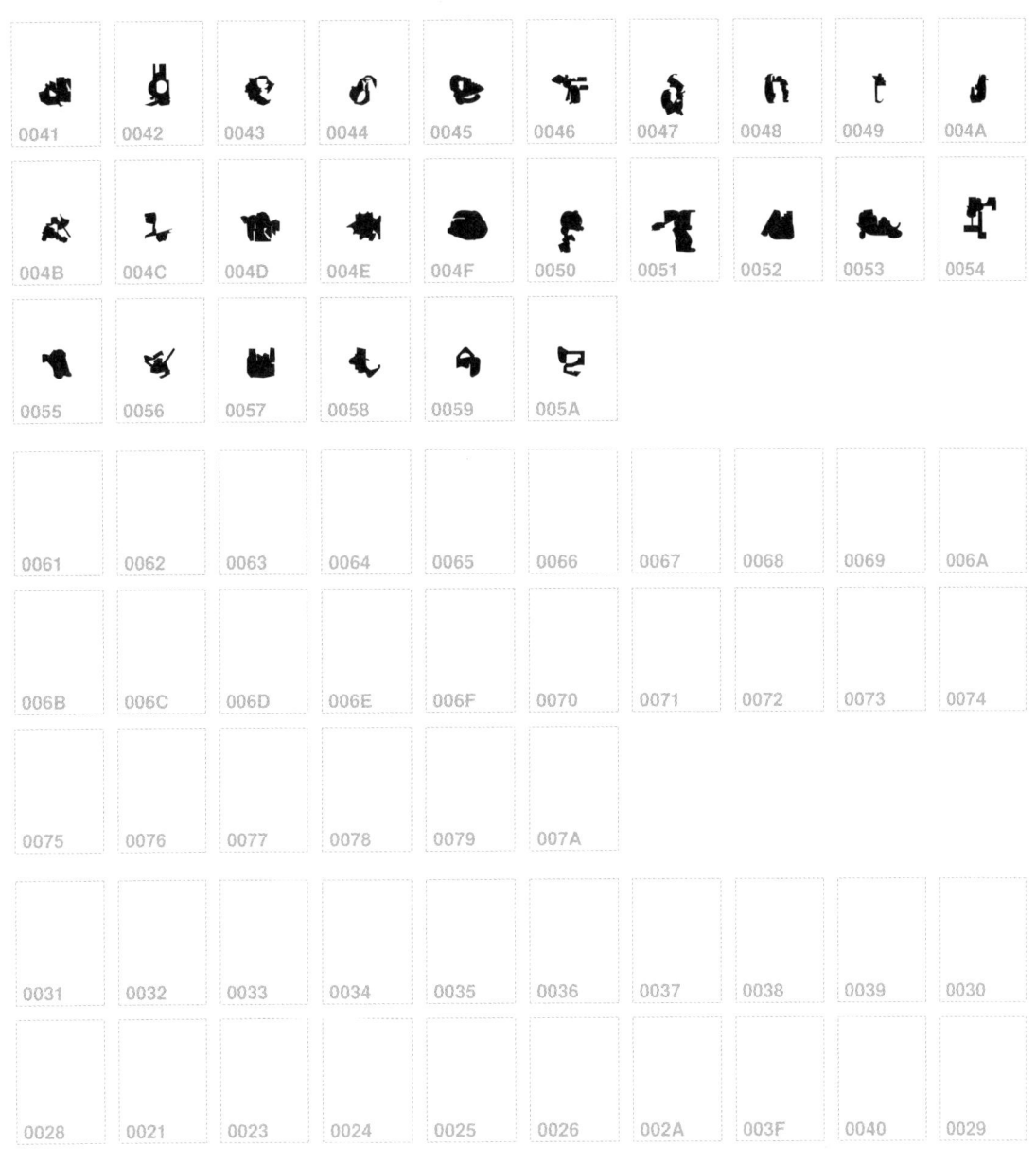

0041	0042	0043	0044	0045	0046	0047	0048	0049	004A
004B	004C	004D	004E	004F	0050	0051	0052	0053	0054
0055	0056	0057	0058	0059	005A				
0061	0062	0063	0064	0065	0066	0067	0068	0069	006A
006B	006C	006D	006E	006F	0070	0071	0072	0073	0074
0075	0076	0077	0078	0079	007A				
0031	0032	0033	0034	0035	0036	0037	0038	0039	0030
0028	0021	0023	0024	0025	0026	002A	003F	0040	0029

0041	0042	0043	0044	0045	0046	0047	0048	0049	004A
004B	004C	004D	004E	004F	0050	0051	0052	0053	0054
0055	0056	0057	0058	0059	005A				
0061	0062	0063	0064	0065	0066	0067	0068	0069	006A
006B	006C	006D	006E	006F	0070	0071	0072	0073	0074
0075	0076	0077	0078	0079	007A				
0031	0032	0033	0034	0035	0036	0037	0038	0039	0030
0028	0021	0023	0024	0025	0026	002A	003F	0040	0029

A	B	C	D	E	F	G	H	I	J
0041	0042	0043	0044	0045	0046	0047	0048	0049	004A
K	L	M	N	O	P	Q	R	S	T
004B	004C	004D	004E	004F	0050	0051	0052	0053	0054
U	V	W	X	Y	Z				
0055	0056	0057	0058	0059	005A				
a	b	c	d	e	f	g	h	i	j
0061	0062	0063	0064	0065	0066	0067	0068	0069	006A
k	l	m	n	o	p	q	r	s	t
006B	006C	006D	006E	006F	0070	0071	0072	0073	0074
u	v	w	x	y	z				
0075	0076	0077	0078	0079	007A				
1	2	3	4	5	6	7	8	9	0
0031	0032	0033	0034	0035	0036	0037	0038	0039	0030
(	!	#	§	%	&	✸	?	@	)
0028	0021	0023	0024	0025	0026	002A	003F	0040	0029

0041	0042	0043	0044	0045	0046	0047	0048	0049	004A
004B	004C	004D	004E	004F	0050	0051	0052	0053	0054
0055	0056	0057	0058	0059	005A				

0061	0062	0063	0064	0065	0066	0067	0068	0069	006A
006B	006C	006D	006E	006F	0070	0071	0072	0073	0074
0075	0076	0077	0078	0079	007A				

0031	0032	0033	0034	0035	0036	0037	0038	0039	0030

(	!	#	$	%	&	*	?	@	)
0028	0021	0023	0024	0025	0026	002A	003F	0040	0029

A	B	C	D	E	F	G	H	I	J
0041	0042	0043	0044	0045	0046	0047	0048	0049	004A
K	L	M	N	O	P	Q	R	S	T
004B	004C	004D	004E	004F	0050	0051	0052	0053	0054
U	V	W	X	Y	Z				
0055	0056	0057	0058	0059	005A				
a	b	c	d	e	f	g	h	i	i
0061	0062	0063	0064	0065	0066	0067	0068	0069	006A
k	l	m	n	o	p	q	r	s	t
006B	006C	006D	006E	006F	0070	0071	0072	0073	0074
u	v	w	x	y	z				
0075	0076	0077	0078	0079	007A				
1	2	3	4	5	6	7	8	9	0
0031	0032	0033	0034	0035	0036	0037	0038	0039	0030
	!				&	#	?		
0028	0021	0023	0024	0025	0026	002A	003F	0040	0029

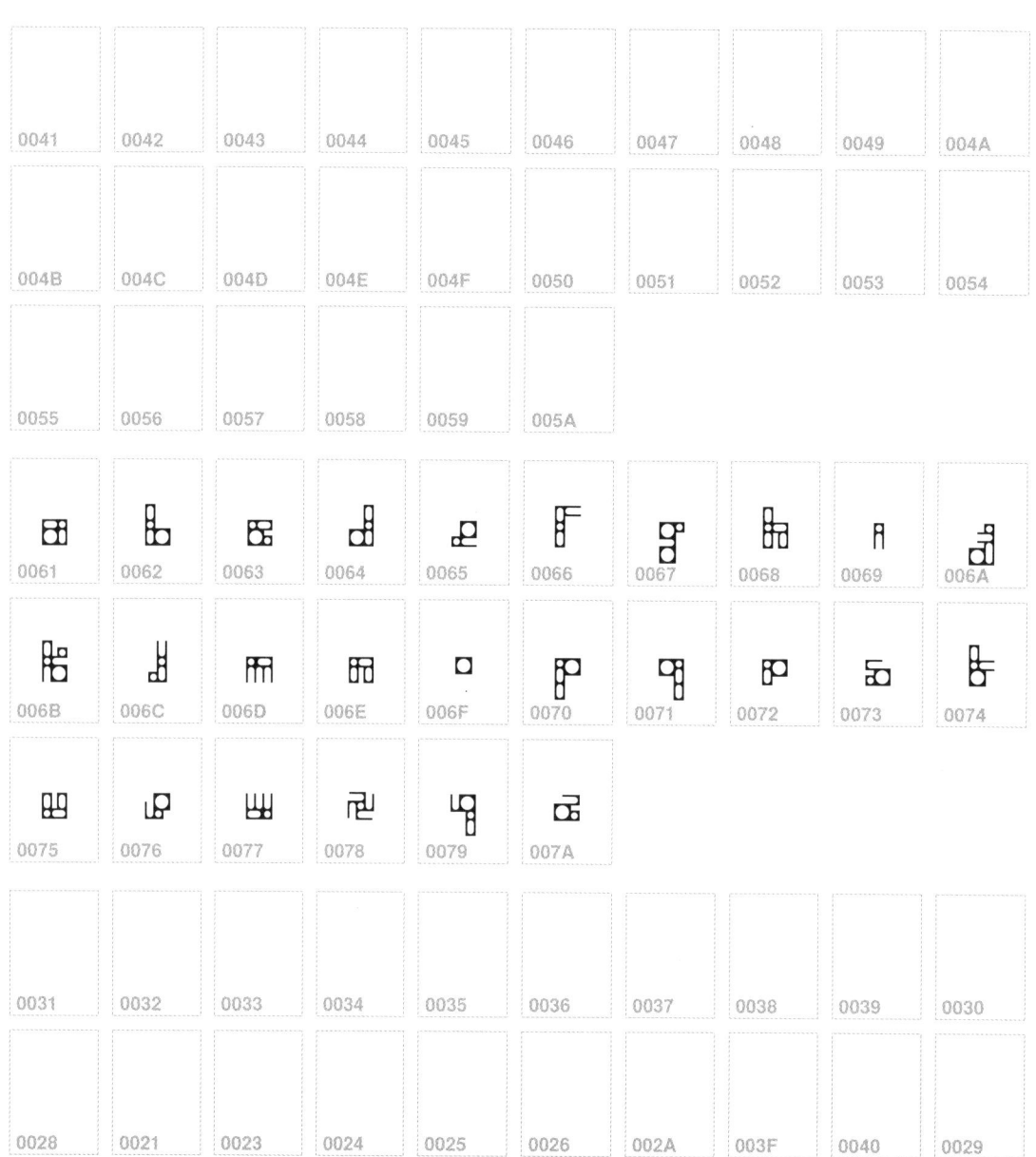

0041	0042	0043	0044	0045	0046	0047	0048	0049	004A
004B	004C	004D	004E	004F	0050	0051	0052	0053	0054
0055	0056	0057	0058	0059	005A				
0061	0062	0063	0064	0065	0066	0067	0068	0069	006A
006B	006C	006D	006E	006F	0070	0071	0072	0073	0074
0075	0076	0077	0078	0079	007A				
0031	0032	0033	0034	0035	0036	0037	0038	0039	0030
0028	0021	0023	0024	0025	0026	002A	003F	0040	0029

0041	0042	0043	0044	0045	0046	0047	0048	0049	004A
004B	004C	004D	004E	004F	0050	0051	0052	0053	0054
0055	0056	0057	0058	0059	005A				
0061	0062	0063	0064	0065	0066	0067	0068	0069	006A
006B	006C	006D	006E	006F	0070	0071	0072	0073	0074
0075	0076	0077	0078	0079	007A				
0031	0032	0033	0034	0035	0036	0037	0038	0039	0030
0028	0021	0023	0024	0025	0026	002A	003F	0040	0029

DATA SHEET: 68

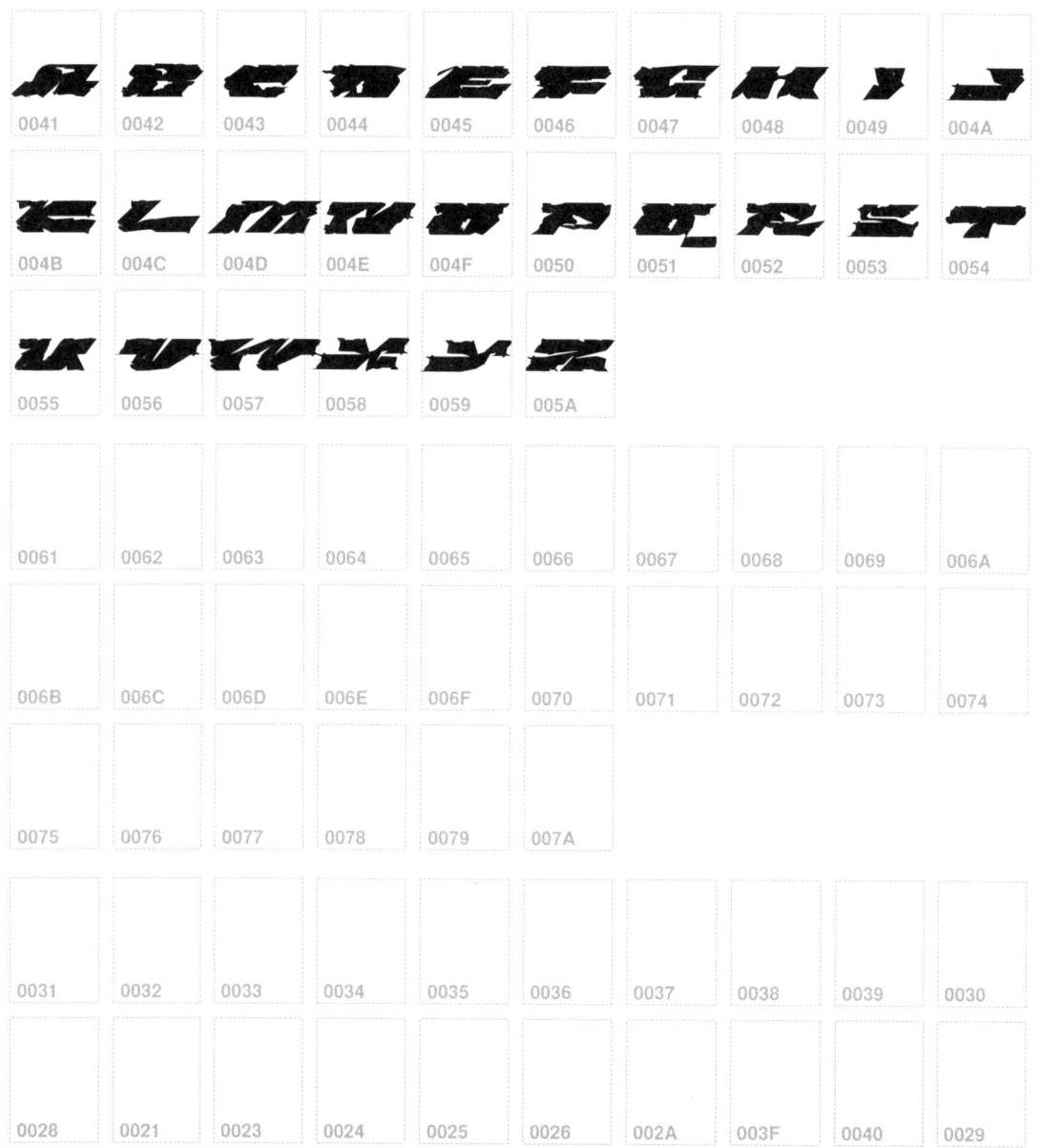

0041	0042	0043	0044	0045	0046	0047	0048	0049	004A
004B	004C	004D	004E	004F	0050	0051	0052	0053	0054
0055	0056	0057	0058	0059	005A				
0061	0062	0063	0064	0065	0066	0067	0068	0069	006A
006B	006C	006D	006E	006F	0070	0071	0072	0073	0074
0075	0076	0077	0078	0079	007A				
0031	0032	0033	0034	0035	0036	0037	0038	0039	0030
0028	0021	0023	0024	0025	0026	002A	003F	0040	0029

DATA SHEET: 72

A	B	C	D	E	F	G	H	I	J
0041	0042	0043	0044	0045	0046	0047	0048	0049	004A
K	L	M	N	O	P	Q	R	S	T
004B	004C	004D	004E	004F	0050	0051	0052	0053	0054
U	V	W	X	Y	Z				
0055	0056	0057	0058	0059	005A				
a	b	c	d	e	f	g	h	i	j
0061	0062	0063	0064	0065	0066	0067	0068	0069	006A
k	l	m	n	o	p	q	r	s	t
006B	006C	006D	006E	006F	0070	0071	0072	0073	0074
u	v	w	x	y	z				
0075	0076	0077	0078	0079	007A				
1	2	3	4	5	6	7	8	9	0
0031	0032	0033	0034	0035	0036	0037	0038	0039	0030
(	!	#	§	%	&	*	?	@	)
0028	0021	0023	0024	0025	0026	002A	003F	0040	0029

TYPEFACE
Gobbble

DESIGNER/S
Simon Bretz,
Hannes Brischke,
Florian Budke

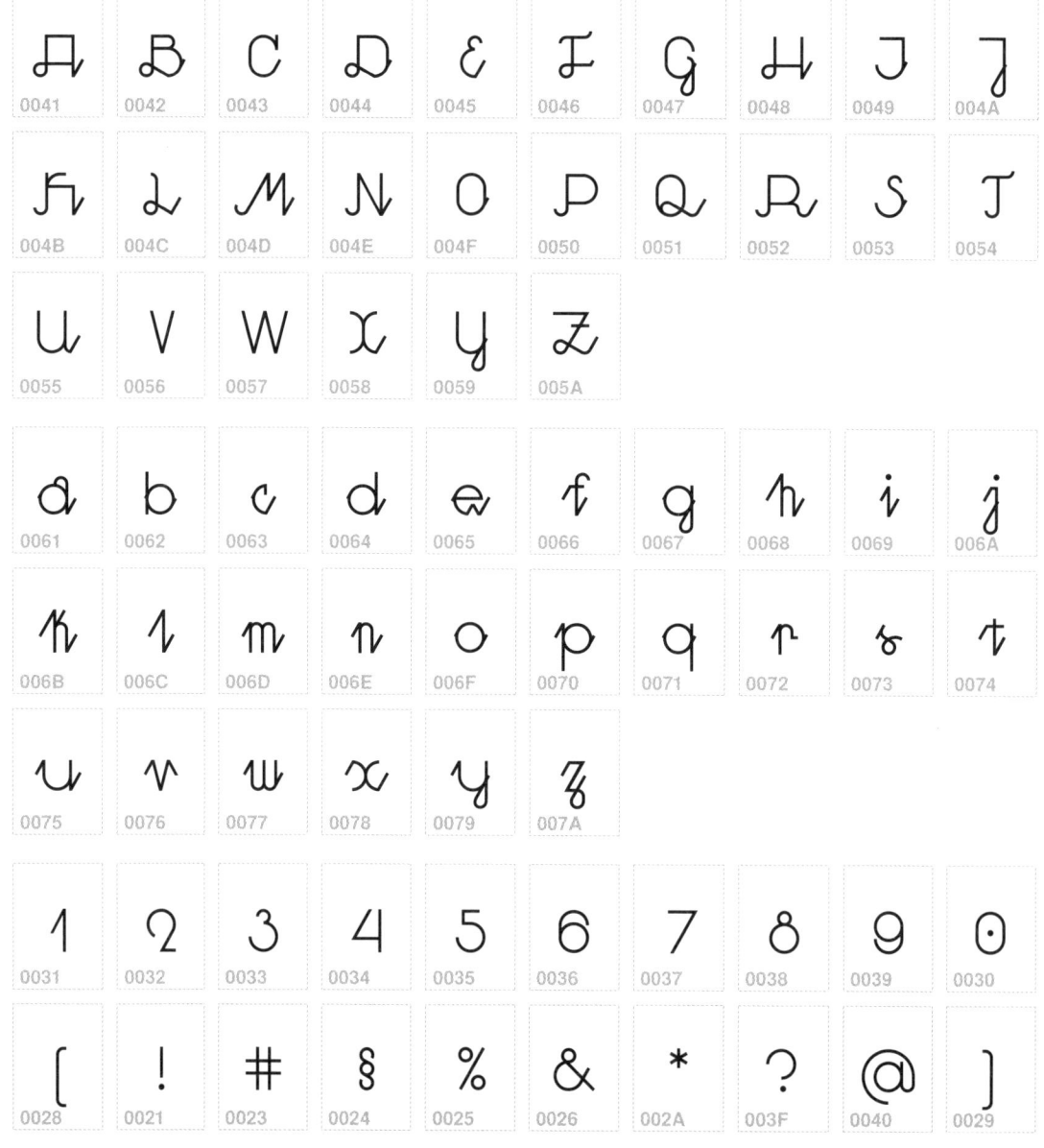

Gosna

Dae Huen Lee

A	B	C	D	E	F	G	H	I	J
0041	0042	0043	0044	0045	0046	0047	0048	0049	004A
K	L	M	N	O	P	Q	R	S	T
004B	004C	004D	004E	004F	0050	0051	0052	0053	0054
U	V	W	X	Y	Z				
0055	0056	0057	0058	0059	005A				
a	b	c	d	e	f	g	h	i	j
0061	0062	0063	0064	0065	0066	0067	0068	0069	006A
k	l	m	n	o	p	q	r	s	t
006B	006C	006D	006E	006F	0070	0071	0072	0073	0074
u	v	w	x	y	z				
0075	0076	0077	0078	0079	007A				
1	2	3	4	5	6	7	8	9	0
0031	0032	0033	0034	0035	0036	0037	0038	0039	0030
(	!	#	§	%	&	*	?	@	)
0028	0021	0023	0024	0025	0026	002A	003F	0040	0029

DATA SHEET: 80

A	B	C	D	E	F	G	H	I	J
0041	0042	0043	0044	0045	0046	0047	0048	0049	004A
K	L	M	N	O	P	Q	R	S	T
004B	004C	004D	004E	004F	0050	0051	0052	0053	0054
U	V	W	X	Y	Z				
0055	0056	0057	0058	0059	005A				
a	b	c	d	e	f	g	h	i	j
0061	0062	0063	0064	0065	0066	0067	0068	0069	006A
k	l	m	n	o	p	q	r	s	t
006B	006C	006D	006E	006F	0070	0071	0072	0073	0074
u	v	w	x	y	z				
0075	0076	0077	0078	0079	007A				
1	2	3	4	5	6	7	8	9	0
0031	0032	0033	0034	0035	0036	0037	0038	0039	0030
[	!	#			&	*	?	@	]
0028	0021	0023	0024	0025	0026	002A	003F	0040	0029

Granturismo

Nathan Laurent

A	B	C	D	E	F	G	H	I	J
0041	0042	0043	0044	0045	0046	0047	0048	0049	004A
K	L	M	N	O	P	Q	R	S	T
004B	004C	004D	004E	004F	0050	0051	0052	0053	0054
U	V	W	X	Y	Z				
0055	0056	0057	0058	0059	005A				
a	b	c	d	e	f	g	h	i	j
0061	0062	0063	0064	0065	0066	0067	0068	0069	006A
k	l	m	n	o	p	q	r	s	t
006B	006C	006D	006E	006F	0070	0071	0072	0073	0074
u	v	w	x	y	z				
0075	0076	0077	0078	0079	007A				
0031	0032	0033	0034	0035	0036	0037	0038	0039	0030
0028	0021	0023	0024	0025	0026	002A	003F	0040	0029

0041	0042	0043	0044	0045	0046	0047	0048	0049	004A
004B	004C	004D	004E	004F	0050	0051	0052	0053	0054
0055	0056	0057	0058	0059	005A				
0061	0062	0063	0064	0065	0066	0067	0068	0069	006A
006B	006C	006D	006E	006F	0070	0071	0072	0073	0074
0075	0076	0077	0078	0079	007A				
0031	0032	0033	0034	0035	0036	0037	0038	0039	0030
0028	0021	0023	0024	0025	0026	002A	003F	0040	0029

0041	0042	0043	0044	0045	0046	0047	0048	0049	004A
004B	004C	004D	004E	004F	0050	0051	0052	0053	0054
0055	0056	0057	0058	0059	005A				
0061	0062	0063	0064	0065	0066	0067	0068	0069	006A
006B	006C	006D	006E	006F	0070	0071	0072	0073	0074
0075	0076	0077	0078	0079	007A				
0031	0032	0033	0034	0035	0036	0037	0038	0039	0030
0028	0021	0023	0024	0025	0026	002A	003F	0040	0029

A	B	C	D	E	F	G	X	I	J
0041	0042	0043	0044	0045	0046	0047	0048	0049	004A
K	L	M	N	O	P	Q	R	S	T
004B	004C	004D	004E	004F	0050	0051	0052	0053	0054
U	V	W	X	Y	Z				
0055	0056	0057	0058	0059	005A				

0061	0062	0063	0064	0065	0066	0067	0068	0069	006A
006B	006C	006D	006E	006F	0070	0071	0072	0073	0074
0075	0076	0077	0078	0079	007A				

1	2	3	4	5	6	7	8	9	0
0031	0032	0033	0034	0035	0036	0037	0038	0039	0030

0028	0021	0023	0024	0025	0026	002A	003F	0040	0029

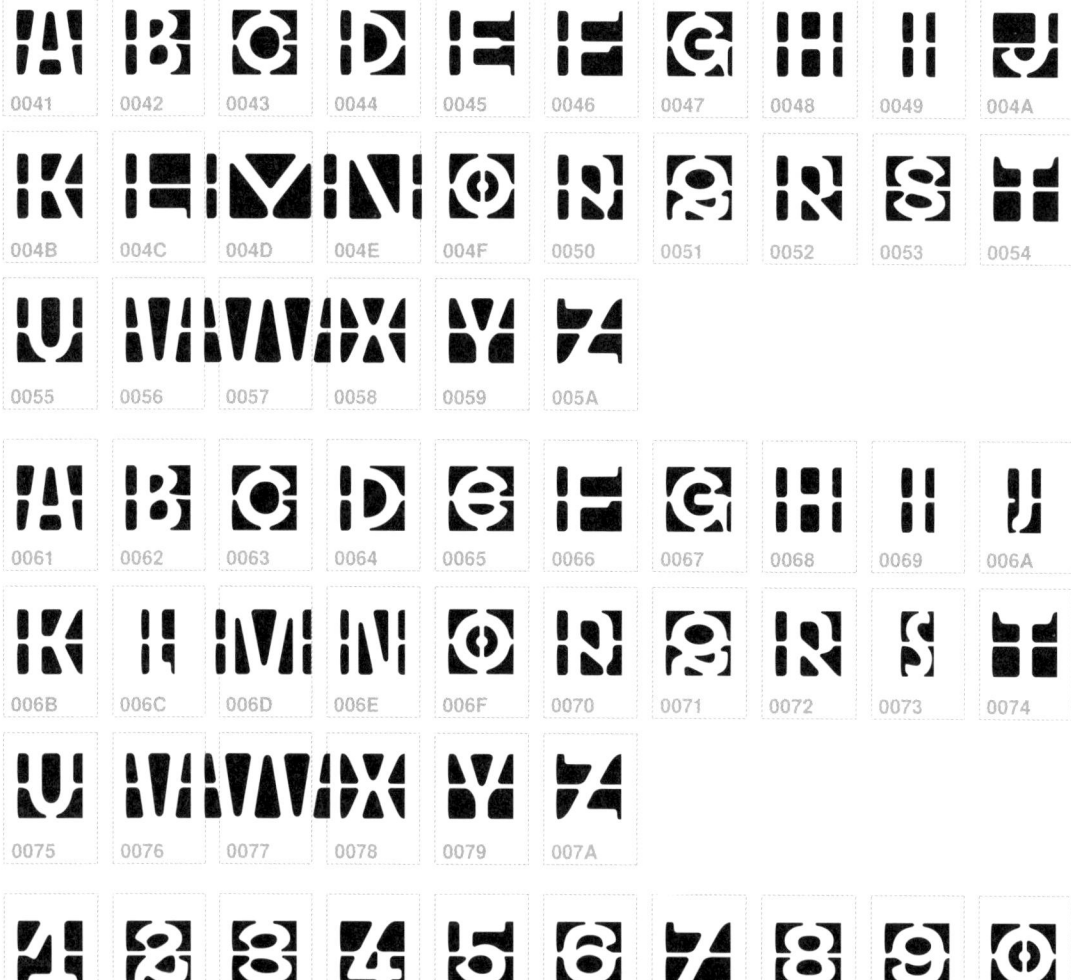

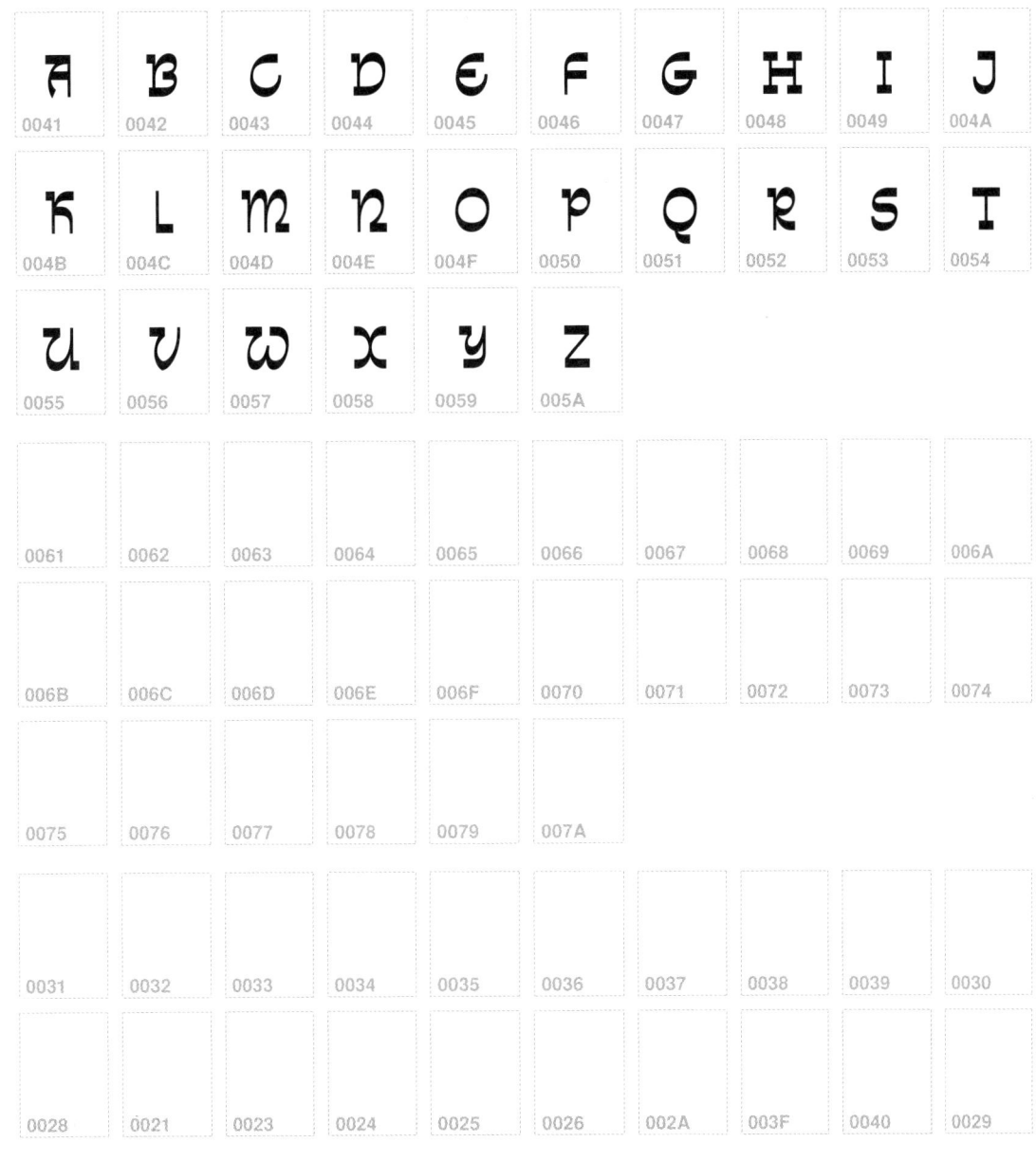

A	B	C	D	E	F	G	H	I	J
0041	0042	0043	0044	0045	0046	0047	0048	0049	004A
K	L	M	N	O	P	Q	R	S	T
004B	004C	004D	004E	004F	0050	0051	0052	0053	0054
U	V	W	X	Y	Z				
0055	0056	0057	0058	0059	005A				
0061	0062	0063	0064	0065	0066	0067	0068	0069	006A
006B	006C	006D	006E	006F	0070	0071	0072	0073	0074
0075	0076	0077	0078	0079	007A				
0031	0032	0033	0034	0035	0036	0037	0038	0039	0030
0028	0021	0023	0024	0025	0026	002A	003F	0040	0029

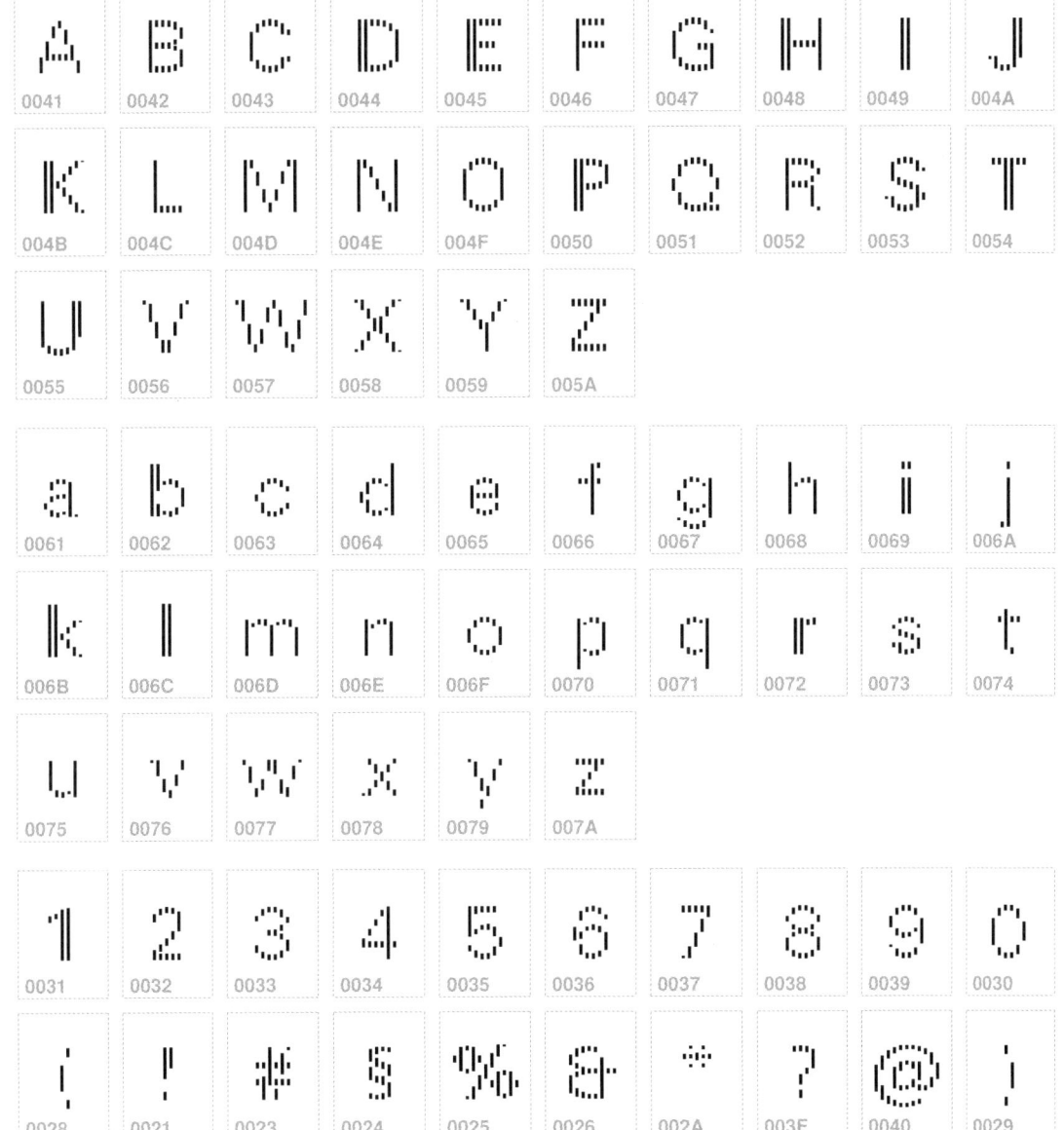

A	B	C	D	E	F	G	H	I	J
0041	0042	0043	0044	0045	0046	0047	0048	0049	004A
K	L	M	N	O	P	Q	R	S	T
004B	004C	004D	004E	004F	0050	0051	0052	0053	0054
U	V	W	X	Y	Z				
0055	0056	0057	0058	0059	005A				
a	b	c	d	e	f	g	h	i	j
0061	0062	0063	0064	0065	0066	0067	0068	0069	006A
k	l	m	n	o	p	q	r	s	t
006B	006C	006D	006E	006F	0070	0071	0072	0073	0074
u	v	w	x	y	z				
0075	0076	0077	0078	0079	007A				
1	2	3	4	5	6	7	8	9	0
0031	0032	0033	0034	0035	0036	0037	0038	0039	0030
(	!	#	$	%	&	*	?	@	)
0028	0021	0023	0024	0025	0026	002A	003F	0040	0029

DATA SHEET: 104

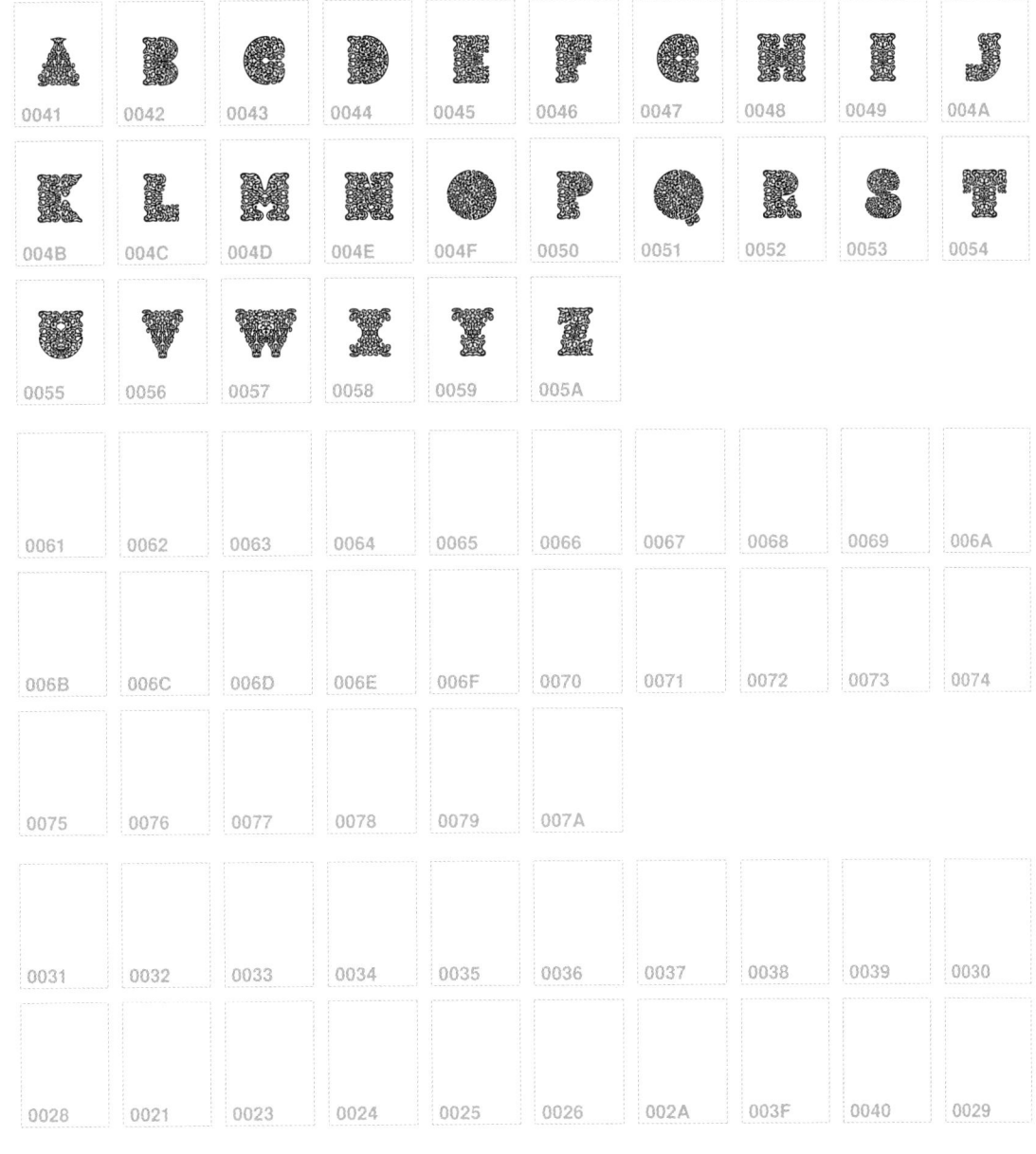

0041 0042 0043 0044 0045 0046 0047 0048 0049 004A

004B 004C 004D 004E 004F 0050 0051 0052 0053 0054

0055 0056 0057 0058 0059 005A

0061 0062 0063 0064 0065 0066 0067 0068 0069 006A

006B 006C 006D 006E 006F 0070 0071 0072 0073 0074

0075 0076 0077 0078 0079 007A

0031 0032 0033 0034 0035 0036 0037 0038 0039 0030

0028 0021 0023 0024 0025 0026 002A 003F 0040 0029

A	B	C	D	E	F	G	H	I	J
0041	0042	0043	0044	0045	0046	0047	0048	0049	004A

K	L	M	N	O	P	Q	R	S	T
004B	004C	004D	004E	004F	0050	0051	0052	0053	0054

U	V	W	X	Y	Z
0055	0056	0057	0058	0059	005A

0061	0062	0063	0064	0065	0066	0067	0068	0069	006A

006B	006C	006D	006E	006F	0070	0071	0072	0073	0074

0075	0076	0077	0078	0079	007A

0031	0032	0033	0034	0035	0036	0037	0038	0039	0030

	!	⚹							
0028	0021	0023	0024	0025	0026	002A	003F	0040	0029

A	B	C	D	E	F	G	H	I	J
0041	0042	0043	0044	0045	0046	0047	0048	0049	004A
K	L	M	N	O	P	Q	R	S	T
004B	004C	004D	004E	004F	0050	0051	0052	0053	0054
U	V	W	X	Y	Z				
0055	0056	0057	0058	0059	005A				
a	b	c	d	e	f	g	h	i	j
0061	0062	0063	0064	0065	0066	0067	0068	0069	006A
k	l	m	n	o	p	q	r	s	t
006B	006C	006D	006E	006F	0070	0071	0072	0073	0074
u	v	w	x	y	z				
0075	0076	0077	0078	0079	007A				
0031	0032	0033	0034	0035	0036	0037	0038	0039	0030
(	!	#	§		&	*	?	@	)
0028	0021	0023	0024	0025	0026	002A	003F	0040	0029

DATA SHEET: 112

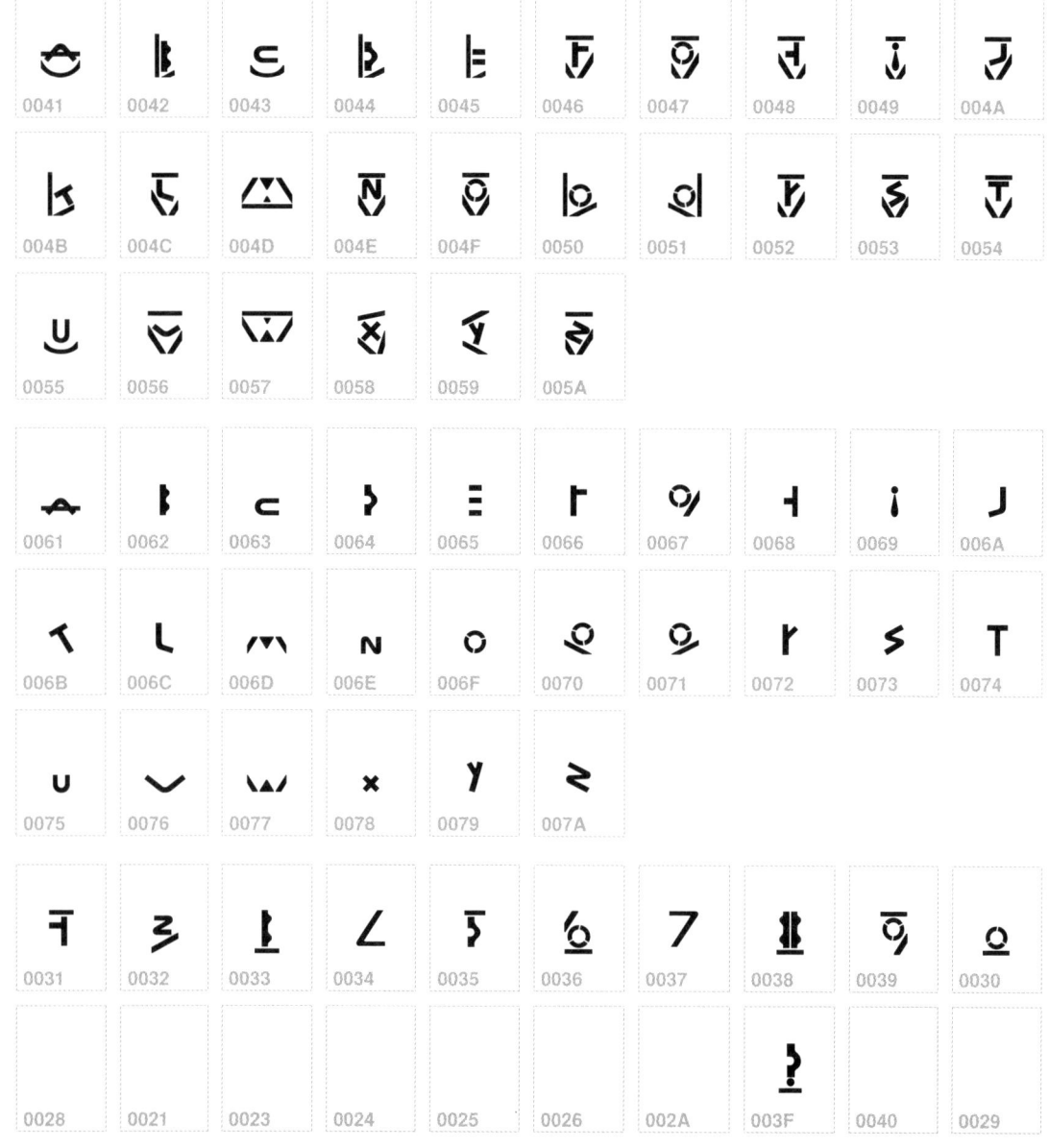

238   **DATA SHEET: 114**

A	B	C	D	E	F	G	H	I	J
0041	0042	0043	0044	0045	0046	0047	0048	0049	004A
K	L	M	N	O	P	Q	R	S	T
004B	004C	004D	004E	004F	0050	0051	0052	0053	0054
U	V	W	X	Y	Z				
0055	0056	0057	0058	0059	005A				
a	b	c	d	e	f	g	h	i	j
0061	0062	0063	0064	0065	0066	0067	0068	0069	006A
k	l	m	n	o	p	q	r	s	t
006B	006C	006D	006E	006F	0070	0071	0072	0073	0074
u	v	w	x	y	z				
0075	0076	0077	0078	0079	007A				
0031	0032	0033	0034	0035	0036	0037	0038	0039	0030
(	!						?		)
0028	0021	0023	0024	0025	0026	002A	003F	0040	0029

DATA SHEET: 116

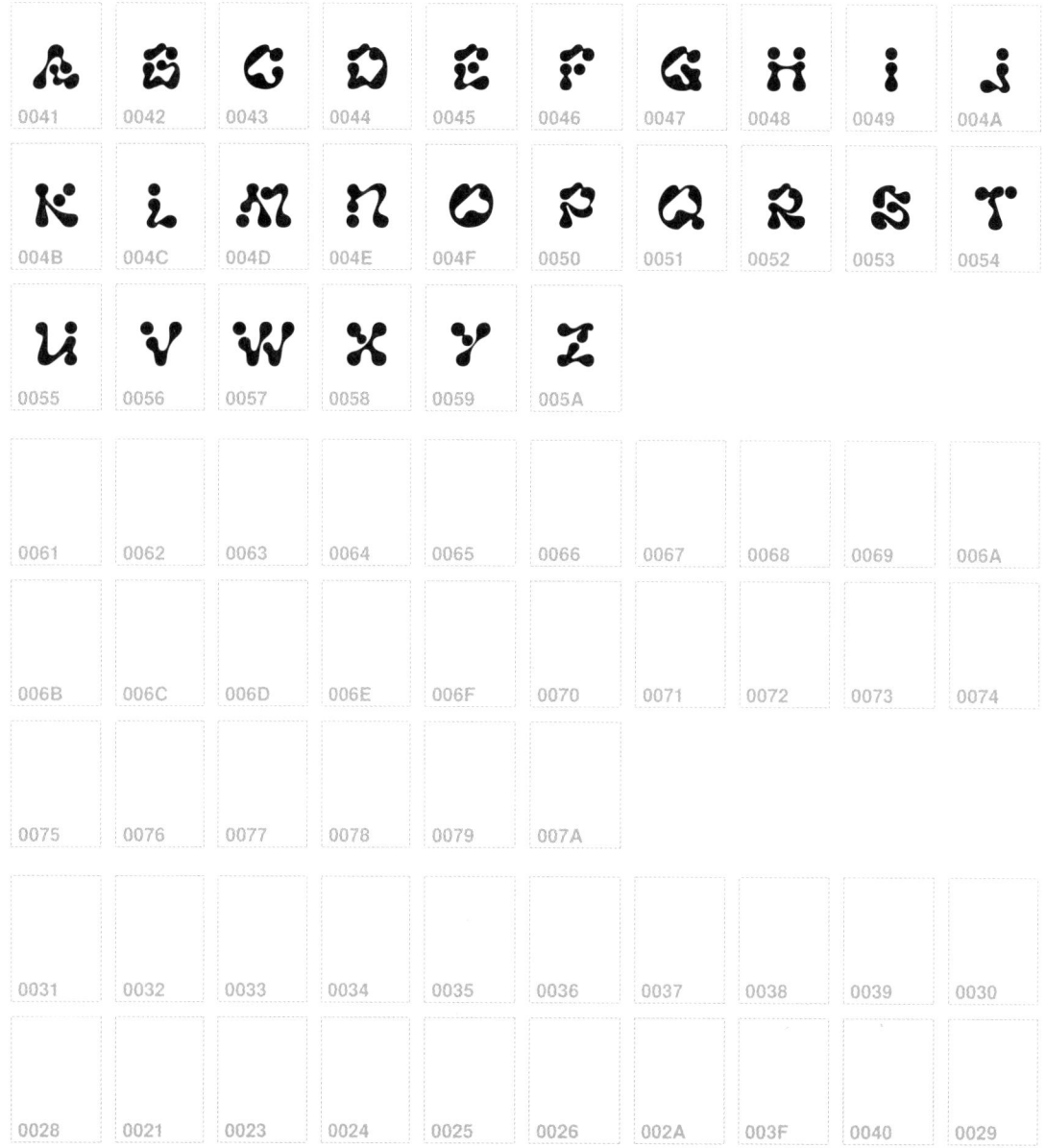

0041	0042	0043	0044	0045	0046	0047	0048	0049	004A
004B	004C	004D	004E	004F	0050	0051	0052	0053	0054
0055	0056	0057	0058	0059	005A				
0061	0062	0063	0064	0065	0066	0067	0068	0069	006A
006B	006C	006D	006E	006F	0070	0071	0072	0073	0074
0075	0076	0077	0078	0079	007A				
0031	0032	0033	0034	0035	0036	0037	0038	0039	0030
0028	0021	0023	0024	0025	0026	002A	003F	0040	0029

A 0041	B 0042	C 0043	D 0044	E 0045	F 0046	G 0047	H 0048	I 0049	J 004A
K 004B	L 004C	M 004D	N 004E	O 004F	P 0050	Q 0051	R 0052	S 0053	T 0054
U 0055	V 0056	W 0057	X 0058	Y 0059	Z 005A				
a 0061	b 0062	c 0063	d 0064	e 0065	f 0066	g 0067	h 0068	i 0069	j 006A
k 006B	l 006C	m 006D	n 006E	o 006F	p 0070	q 0071	r 0072	s 0073	t 0074
u 0075	v 0076	w 0077	x 0078	y 0079	z 007A				
1 0031	2 0032	3 0033	4 0034	5 0035	6 0036	7 0037	8 0038	9 0039	0 0030
0028	0021	0023	0024	0025	0026	002A	003F	0040	0029

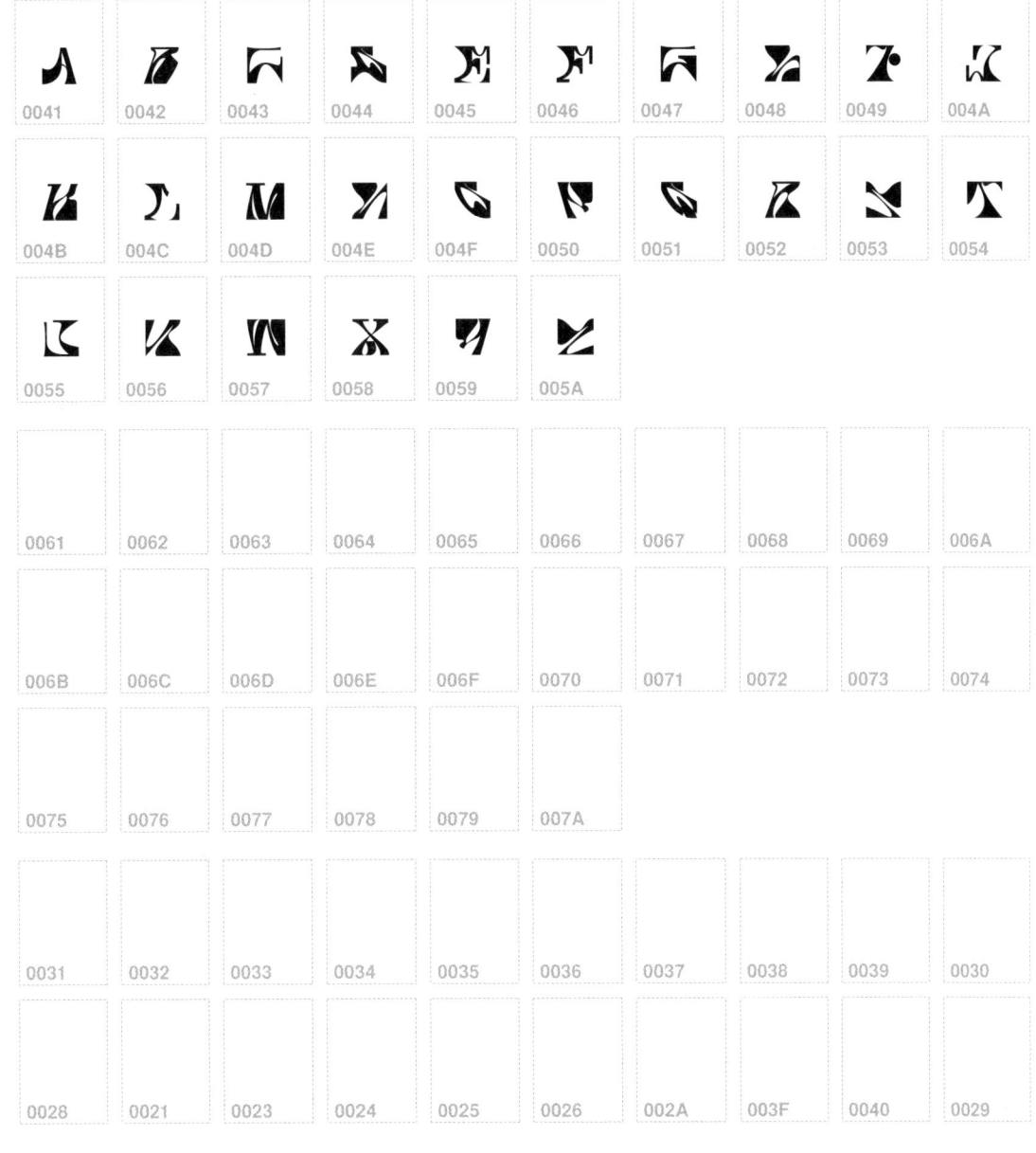

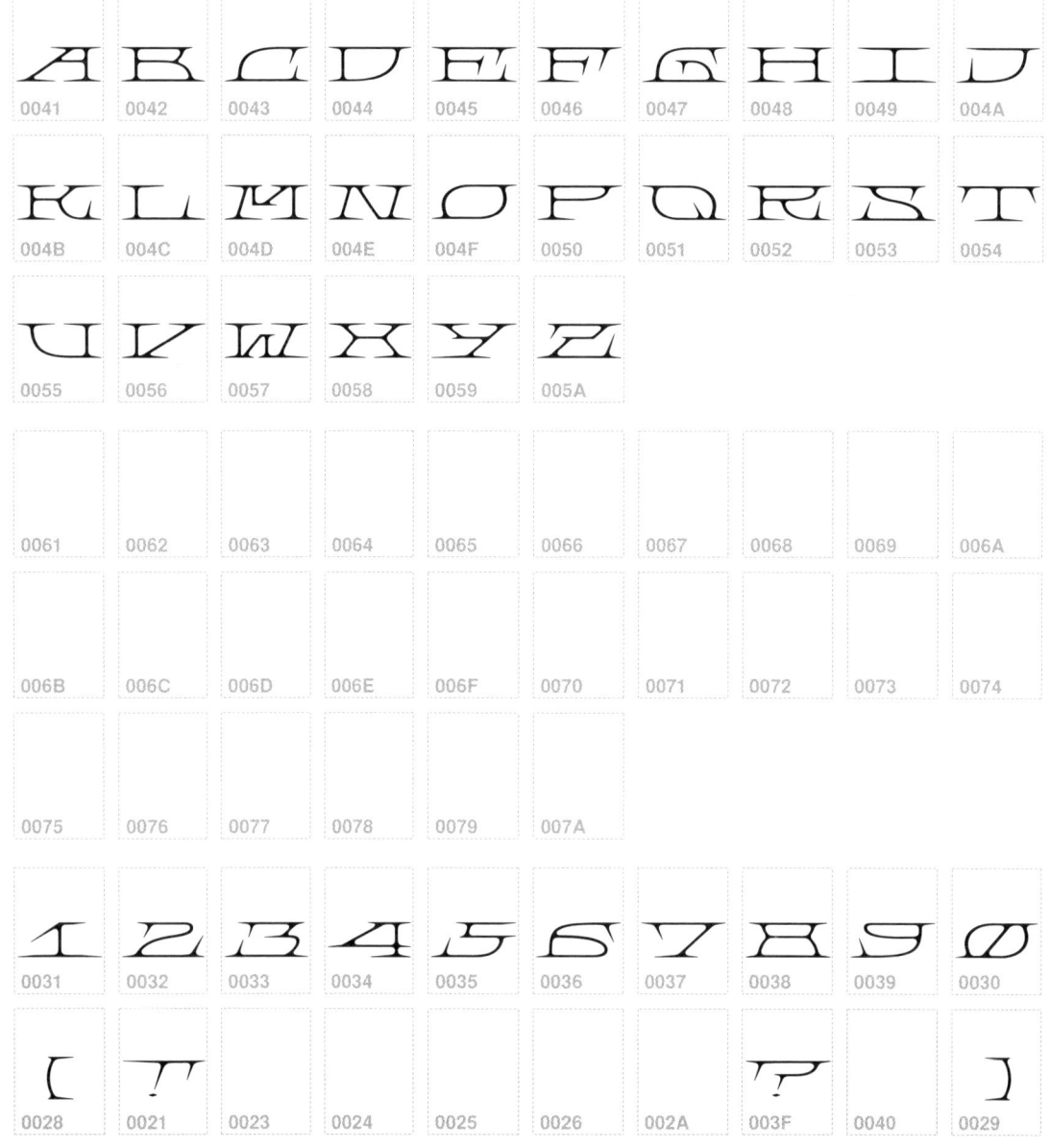

A	B	C	D	E	F	G	H	I	J
0041	0042	0043	0044	0045	0046	0047	0048	0049	004A

K	L	M	N	O	P	Q	R	S	T
004B	004C	004D	004E	004F	0050	0051	0052	0053	0054

U	V	W	X	Y	Z
0055	0056	0057	0058	0059	005A

a	b	c	d	e	f	g	h	i	j
0061	0062	0063	0064	0065	0066	0067	0068	0069	006A

k	l	m	n	o	p	q	r	s	t
006B	006C	006D	006E	006F	0070	0071	0072	0073	0074

u	v	w	x	y	z
0075	0076	0077	0078	0079	007A

1	2	3	4	5	6	7	8	9	0
0031	0032	0033	0034	0035	0036	0037	0038	0039	0030

(	!	#					?		)
0028	0021	0023	0024	0025	0026	002A	003F	0040	0029

DATA SHEET: 128

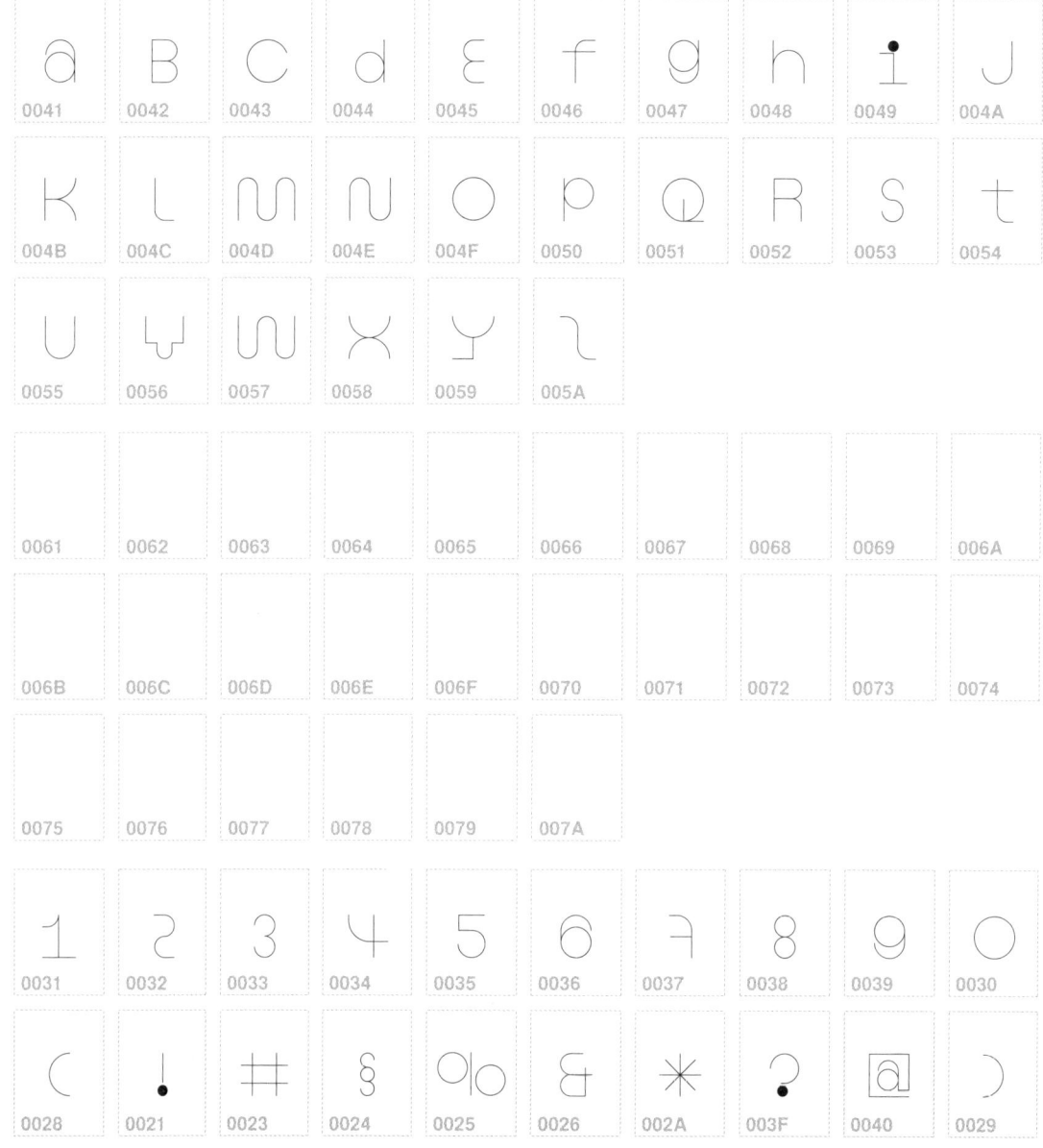

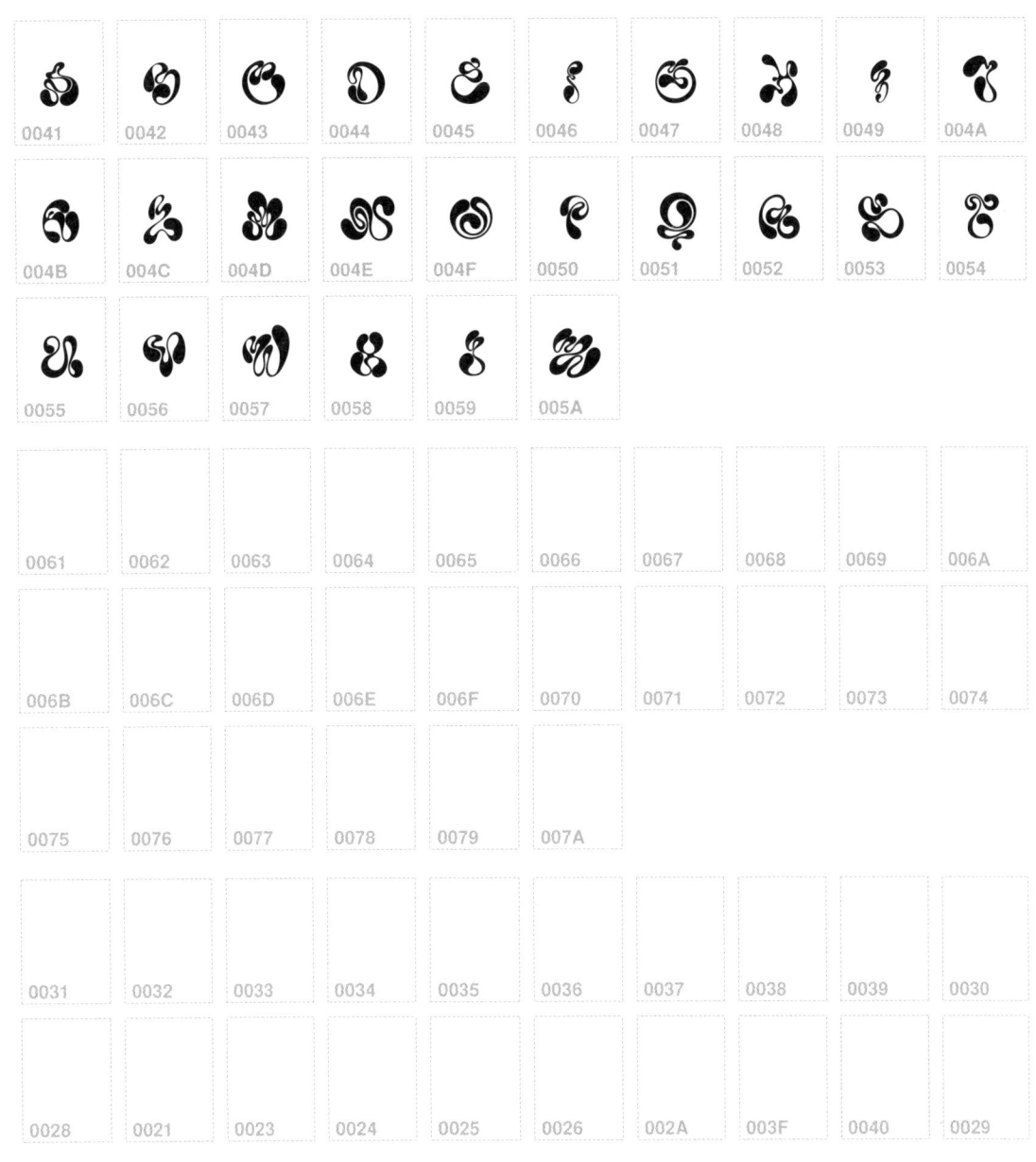

0041	0042	0043	0044	0045	0046	0047	0048	0049	004A
004B	004C	004D	004E	004F	0050	0051	0052	0053	0054
0055	0056	0057	0058	0059	005A				
0061	0062	0063	0064	0065	0066	0067	0068	0069	006A
006B	006C	006D	006E	006F	0070	0071	0072	0073	0074
0075	0076	0077	0078	0079	007A				
0031	0032	0033	0034	0035	0036	0037	0038	0039	0030
0028	0021	0023	0024	0025	0026	002A	003F	0040	0029

DATA SHEET: 136

A	*B*	*C*	*D*	*E*	*F*	*G*	*H*	*I*	*J*
0041	0042	0043	0044	0045	0046	0047	0048	0049	004A
K	*L*	*M*	*N*	*O*	*P*	*Q*	*R*	*S*	*T*
004B	004C	004D	004E	004F	0050	0051	0052	0053	0054
U	*V*	*W*	*X*	*Y*	*Z*				
0055	0056	0057	0058	0059	005A				
a	*b*	*c*	*d*	*e*	*f*	*g*	*h*	*i*	*j*
0061	0062	0063	0064	0065	0066	0067	0068	0069	006A
k	*l*	*m*	*n*	*o*	*p*	*q*	*r*	*s*	*t*
006B	006C	006D	006E	006F	0070	0071	0072	0073	0074
u	*v*	*w*	*x*	*y*	*z*				
0075	0076	0077	0078	0079	007A				
1	*2*	*3*	*4*	*5*	*6*	*7*	*8*	*9*	*0*
0031	0032	0033	0034	0035	0036	0037	0038	0039	0030
0028	0021	0023	0024	0025	0026	002A	003F	0040	0029

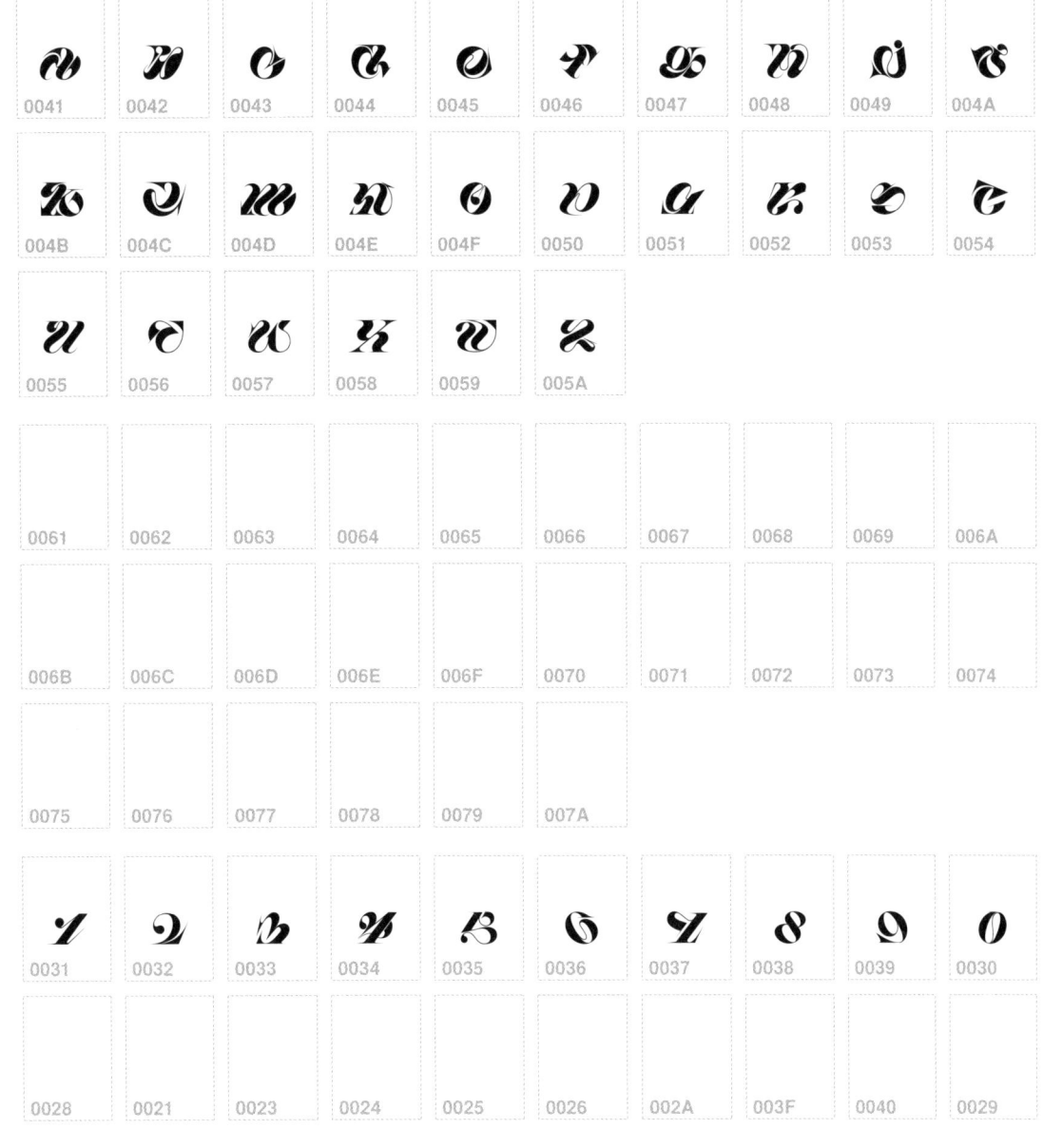

0041	0042	0043	0044	0045	0046	0047	0048	0049	004A
004B	004C	004D	004E	004F	0050	0051	0052	0053	0054
0055	0056	0057	0058	0059	005A				
0061	0062	0063	0064	0065	0066	0067	0068	0069	006A
006B	006C	006D	006E	006F	0070	0071	0072	0073	0074
0075	0076	0077	0078	0079	007A				
0031	0032	0033	0034	0035	0036	0037	0038	0039	0030
0028	0021	0023	0024	0025	0026	002A	003F	0040	0029

A	B	C	D	E	F	G	H	I	J
0041	0042	0043	0044	0045	0046	0047	0048	0049	004A
K	L	M	N	O	P	Q	R	S	T
004B	004C	004D	004E	004F	0050	0051	0052	0053	0054
U	V	W	X	Y	Z				
0055	0056	0057	0058	0059	005A				
a	b	c	d	e	f	g	h	i	j
0061	0062	0063	0064	0065	0066	0067	0068	0069	006A
k	l	m	n	o	p	q	r	s	t
006B	006C	006D	006E	006F	0070	0071	0072	0073	0074
u	v	w	x	y	z				
0075	0076	0077	0078	0079	007A				
1	2	3	4	5	6	7	8	9	0
0031	0032	0033	0034	0035	0036	0037	0038	0039	0030
(	!	#	§	%	&	*	?	@	)
0028	0021	0023	0024	0025	0026	002A	003F	0040	0029

DATA SHEET: 142

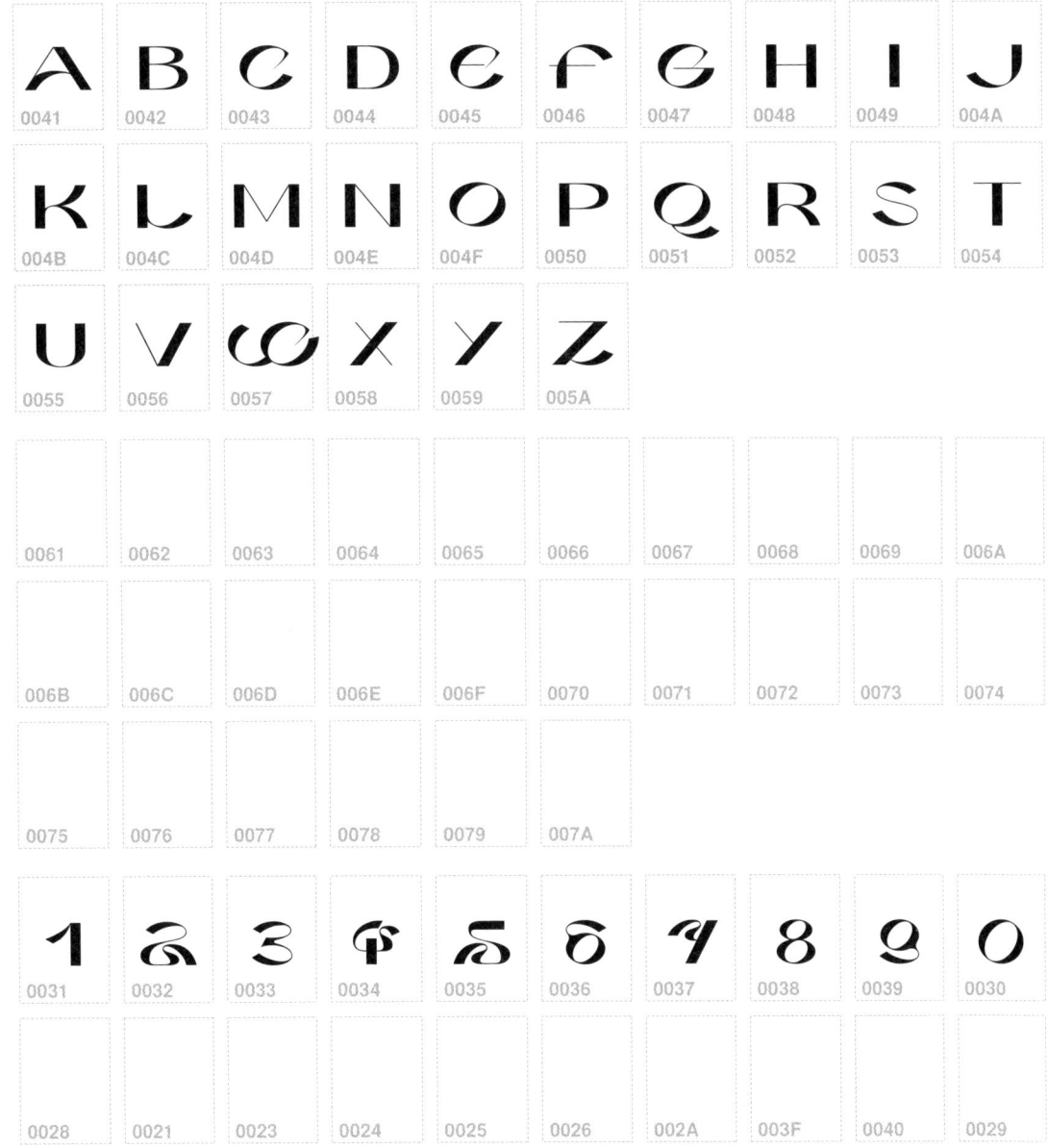

0041	0042	0043	0044	0045	0046	0047	0048	0049	004A
004B	004C	004D	004E	004F	0050	0051	0052	0053	0054
0055	0056	0057	0058	0059	005A				
0061	0062	0063	0064	0065	0066	0067	0068	0069	006A
006B	006C	006D	006E	006F	0070	0071	0072	0073	0074
0075	0076	0077	0078	0079	007A				
0031	0032	0033	0034	0035	0036	0037	0038	0039	0030
0028	0021	0023	0024	0025	0026	002A	003F	0040	0029

0041	0042	0043	0044	0045	0046	0047	0048	0049	004A
004B	004C	004D	004E	004F	0050	0051	0052	0053	0054
0055	0056	0057	0058	0059	005A				
0061	0062	0063	0064	0065	0066	0067	0068	0069	006A
006B	006C	006D	006E	006F	0070	0071	0072	0073	0074
0075	0076	0077	0078	0079	007A				
0031	0032	0033	0034	0035	0036	0037	0038	0039	0030
0028	0021	0023	0024	0025	0026	002A	003F	0040	0029

A	B	C	D	E	F	G	H	I	J
0041	0042	0043	0044	0045	0046	0047	0048	0049	004A

K	L	M	N	O	P	Q	R	S	T
004B	004C	004D	004E	004F	0050	0051	0052	0053	0054

U	V	W	X	Y	Z
0055	0056	0057	0058	0059	005A

0061	0062	0063	0064	0065	0066	0067	0068	0069	006A

006B	006C	006D	006E	006F	0070	0071	0072	0073	0074

0075	0076	0077	0078	0079	007A

1	2	3	4	5	6	7	8	9	0
0031	0032	0033	0034	0035	0036	0037	0038	0039	0030

0028	0021	0023	0024	0025	0026	002A	003F	0040	0029

a	*b*	*c*	*d*	*e*	*f*	*g*	*h*	*i*	*j*
0041	0042	0043	0044	0045	0046	0047	0048	0049	004A
k	*l*	*m*	*n*	*o*	*p*	*q*	*r*	*s*	*t*
004B	004C	004D	004E	004F	0050	0051	0052	0053	0054
u	*v*	*w*	*x*	*y*	*z*				
0055	0056	0057	0058	0059	005A				
0061	0062	0063	0064	0065	0066	0067	0068	0069	006A
006B	006C	006D	006E	006F	0070	0071	0072	0073	0074
0075	0076	0077	0078	0079	007A				
1	2	3	4	5	6	7	8	9	0
0031	0032	0033	0034	0035	0036	0037	0038	0039	0030
(	!	#			&	*	?	@	)
0028	0021	0023	0024	0025	0026	002A	003F	0040	0029

0041	0042	0043	0044	0045	0046	0047	0048	0049	004A
004B	004C	004D	004E	004F	0050	0051	0052	0053	0054
0055	0056	0057	0058	0059	005A				
0061	0062	0063	0064	0065	0066	0067	0068	0069	006A
006B	006C	006D	006E	006F	0070	0071	0072	0073	0074
0075	0076	0077	0078	0079	007A				
0031	0032	0033	0034	0035	0036	0037	0038	0039	0030
0028	0021	0023	0024	0025	0026	002A	003F	0040	0029

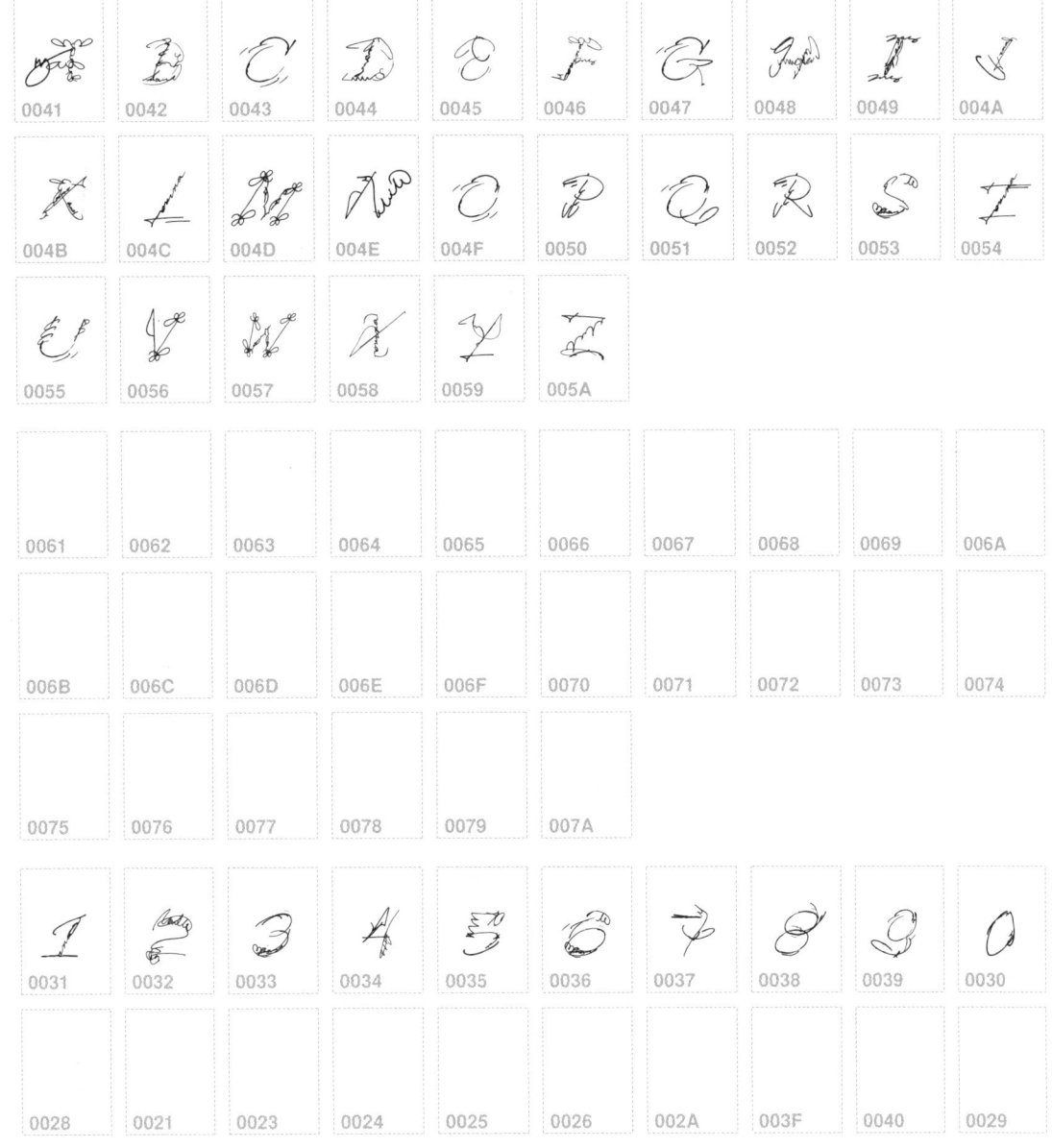

0041	0042	0043	0044	0045	0046	0047	0048	0049	004A
004B	004C	004D	004E	004F	0050	0051	0052	0053	0054
0055	0056	0057	0058	0059	005A				
0061	0062	0063	0064	0065	0066	0067	0068	0069	006A
006B	006C	006D	006E	006F	0070	0071	0072	0073	0074
0075	0076	0077	0078	0079	007A				
0031	0032	0033	0034	0035	0036	0037	0038	0039	0030
0028	0021	0023	0024	0025	0026	002A	003F	0040	0029

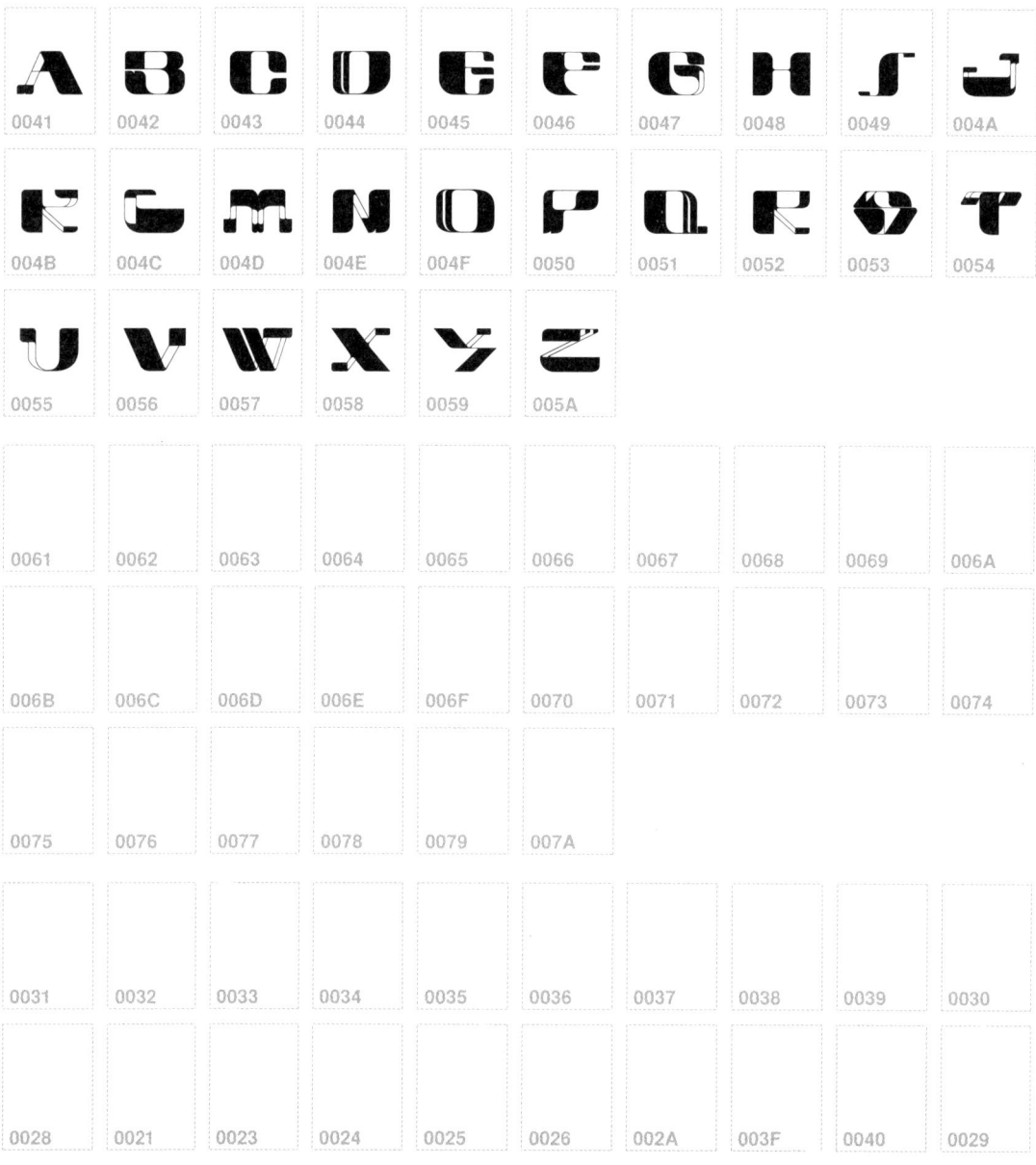

A	*B*	*C*	*D*	*E*	*F*	*G*	*H*	*I*	*J*
0041	0042	0043	0044	0045	0046	0047	0048	0049	004A
K	*L*	*M*	*N*	*O*	*P*	*Q*	*R*	*S*	*T*
004B	004C	004D	004E	004F	0050	0051	0052	0053	0054
U	*V*	*W*	*X*	*Y*	*Z*				
0055	0056	0057	0058	0059	005A				
a	*b*	*c*	*d*	*e*	*f*	*g*	*h*	*i*	*j*
0061	0062	0063	0064	0065	0066	0067	0068	0069	006A
k	*l*	*m*	*n*	*o*	*p*	*q*	*r*	*s*	*t*
006B	006C	006D	006E	006F	0070	0071	0072	0073	0074
u	*v*	*w*	*x*	*y*	*z*				
0075	0076	0077	0078	0079	007A				
1	*2*								*0*
0031	0032	0033	0034	0035	0036	0037	0038	0039	0030
0028	0021	0023	0024	0025	0026	002A	003F	0040	0029

DATA SHEET: 160

Tangerine

Emilie Vizcano

A	B	C	D	E	F	G	H	I	J
0041	0042	0043	0044	0045	0046	0047	0048	0049	004A
K	L	M	N	O	P	Q	R	S	T
004B	004C	004D	004E	004F	0050	0051	0052	0053	0054
U	V	W	X	Y	Z				
0055	0056	0057	0058	0059	005A				
a	b	c	d	e	f	g	h	i	j
0061	0062	0063	0064	0065	0066	0067	0068	0069	006A
k	l	m	n	o	p	q	r	s	t
006B	006C	006D	006E	006F	0070	0071	0072	0073	0074
u	v	w	x	y	z				
0075	0076	0077	0078	0079	007A				
1	2	3	4	5	6	7	8	9	0
0031	0032	0033	0034	0035	0036	0037	0038	0039	0030
(	!		§		&		?		)
0028	0021	0023	0024	0025	0026	002A	003F	0040	0029

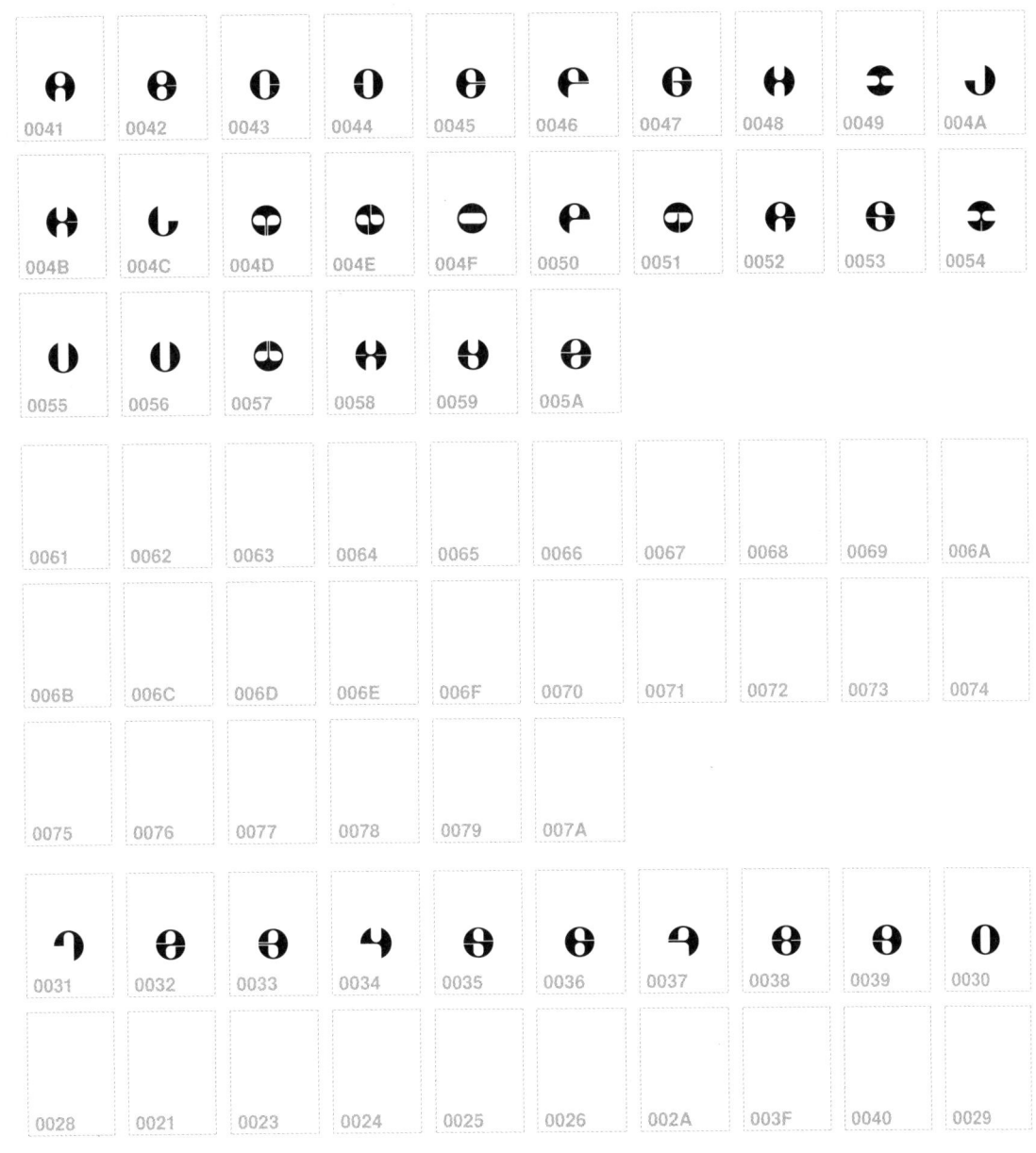

DATA SHEET: 164

A	B	C	D	E	F	G	H	I	J
0041	0042	0043	0044	0045	0046	0047	0048	0049	004A
K	L	M	N	O	P	Q	R	S	T
004B	004C	004D	004E	004F	0050	0051	0052	0053	0054
U	V	W	X	Y	Z				
0055	0056	0057	0058	0059	005A				

0061	0062	0063	0064	0065	0066	0067	0068	0069	006A
006B	006C	006D	006E	006F	0070	0071	0072	0073	0074
0075	0076	0077	0078	0079	007A				

1	2	3	4	5	6	7	8	9	0
0031	0032	0033	0034	0035	0036	0037	0038	0039	0030
(	!						?		)
0028	0021	0023	0024	0025	0026	002A	003F	0040	0029

DATA SHEET: 166

A	B	C	D	E	F	G	H	I	J
0041	0042	0043	0044	0045	0046	0047	0048	0049	004A
K	L	M	N	O	P	Q	R	S	T
004B	004C	004D	004E	004F	0050	0051	0052	0053	0054
U	V	W	X	Y	Z				
0055	0056	0057	0058	0059	005A				
a	b	c	d	e	f	g	h	i	j
0061	0062	0063	0064	0065	0066	0067	0068	0069	006A
k	l	m	n	o	p	q	r	s	t
006B	006C	006D	006E	006F	0070	0071	0072	0073	0074
u	v	w	x	y	z				
0075	0076	0077	0078	0079	007A				
1	2	3	4	5	6	7	8	9	0
0031	0032	0033	0034	0035	0036	0037	0038	0039	0030
(	!	#	§	%	&	*	?	@	)
0028	0021	0023	0024	0025	0026	002A	003F	0040	0029

DATA SHEET: 168

A	B	C	D	E	F	G	H	I	J
0041	0042	0043	0044	0045	0046	0047	0048	0049	004A

K	L	M	N	O	P	Q	R	S	T
004B	004C	004D	004E	004F	0050	0051	0052	0053	0054

U	V	W	X	Y	Z
0055	0056	0057	0058	0059	005A

a	b	c	d	e	f	g	h	i	j
0061	0062	0063	0064	0065	0066	0067	0068	0069	006A

k	l	m	n	o	p	q	r	s	t
006B	006C	006D	006E	006F	0070	0071	0072	0073	0074

u	v	w	x	y	z
0075	0076	0077	0078	0079	007A

1	2	3	4	5	6	7	8	9	0
0031	0032	0033	0034	0035	0036	0037	0038	0039	0030

(	!	#	§	%	&	*	?	@	)
0028	0021	0023	0024	0025	0026	002A	003F	0040	0029

DATA SHEET: 170

0041	0042	0043	0044	0045	0046	0047	0048	0049	004A
004B	004C	004D	004E	004F	0050	0051	0052	0053	0054
0055	0056	0057	0058	0059	005A				
0061	0062	0063	0064	0065	0066	0067	0068	0069	006A
006B	006C	006D	006E	006F	0070	0071	0072	0073	0074
0075	0076	0077	0078	0079	007A				
0031	0032	0033	0034	0035	0036	0037	0038	0039	0030
0028	0021	0023	0024	0025	0026	002A	003F	0040	0029

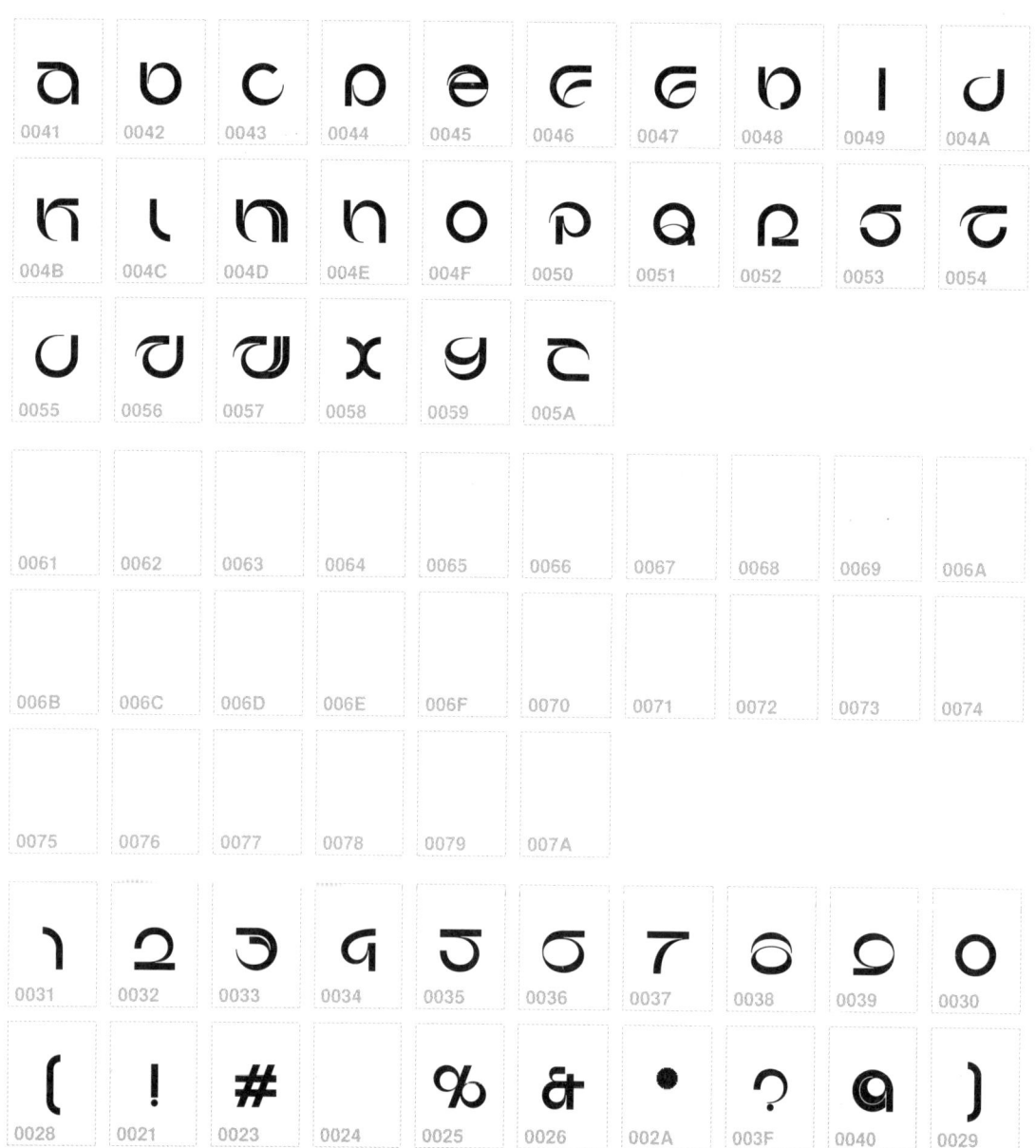

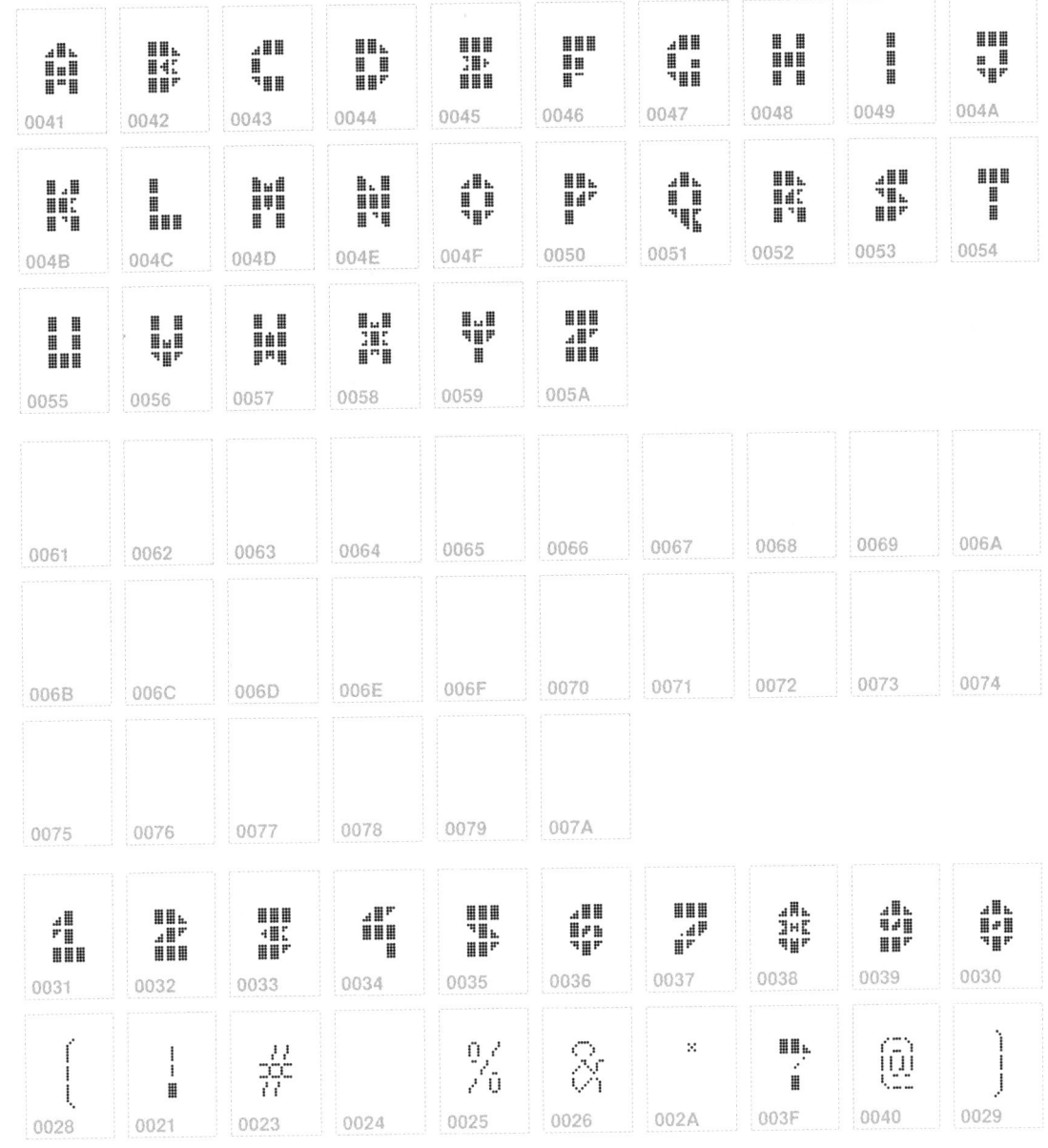

DATA SHEET: 176

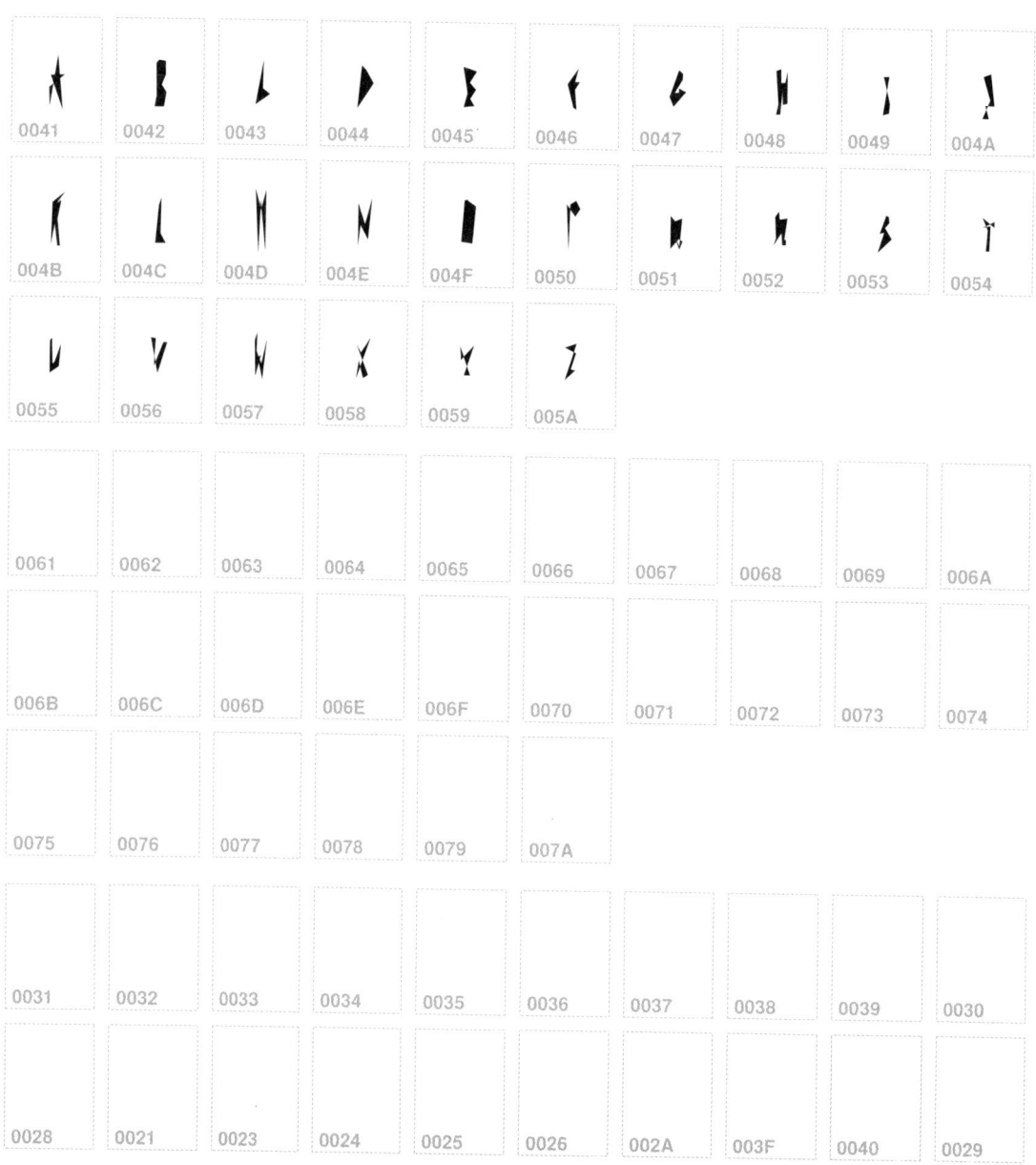

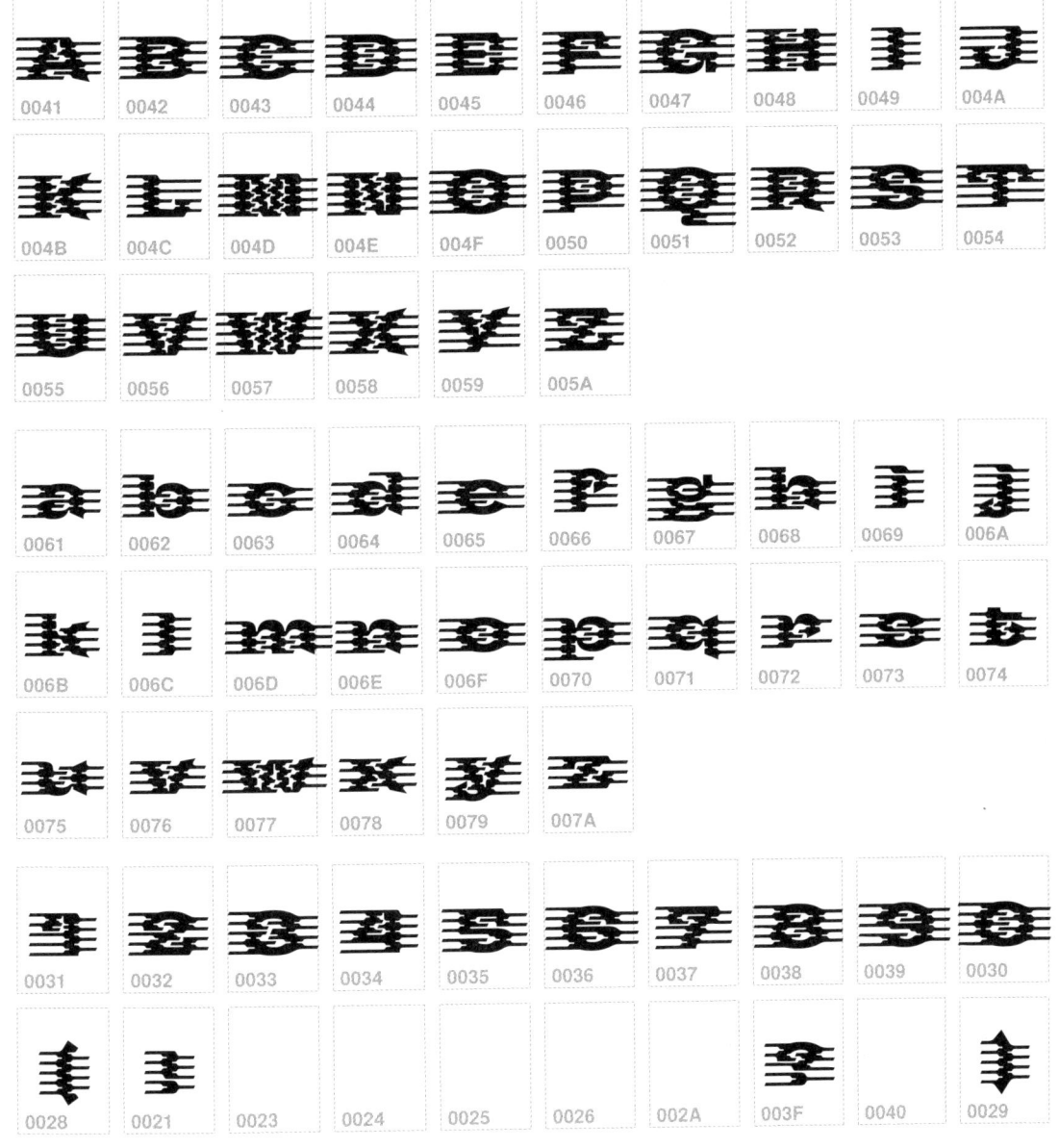

NEW AESTHETIC 3
A Collection of Experimental and Independent Type Design

EDITORS
Leonhard Laupichler
Sophia Brinkgerd

PUBLISHER
Sorry Press®
sorry-press.com

CONTENT DIRECTOR
Lukas Kubina

DESIGN DIRECTION
Wiegand von Hartmann
Moritz Wiegand, Sophie von Hartmann

PRODUCTION
KOPA Lithuania

Printed in Lithuania
ISBN 978-3-9820440-9-5